When I grow up

Structured experiences for expanding male and female roles

Vol. I

**The Early
And Middle
School Years**

By Michelle Kavanaugh, Ph.D

Design and layout: Susan Fritts
Mechanical art: Ellen Skipper

humanics

P. O. Box 7447
Atlanta, Georgia 30309

PRINTED IN THE UNITED STATES OF AMERICA
ISBN 0-89334-016-2

When I grow up vol. I

Contents

General Introduction

The exercises in this book are for students at all developmental levels, pre-kindergarten through late adolescence, and for the adults who work with them. Each activity is supported by the assumption that providing opportunities for both sexes to reach their full potential requires sexual equality and the elimination of sexual stereotyping. Strict and narrow definitions of sexual options are rejected as limiting human options. The goal for this book, therefore, is to provide activities which will assist people in the helping professions support young people as they strive to achieve a positive self-concept.

How does one develop a positive self-concept? Your self-concept, and those of the young people with whom you work, emerged gradually out of self-awareness. At about age three there was a "you" inside yourself who began to observe you, evaluate its observations, and develop plans and hopes for the "you" of the future on the basis of the evaluations. You can verify this by searching your mind for your earliest memories. Most of us don't find any strong memories before age three. This is because our self-concept had not yet become integrated before then.

Now this young and tender "you" inside was neutral to begin with but it didn't stay that way long. It soon began to applaud, or blush, and perhaps even kick at the you it observed. Of course you had to have help initially in learning this judgemental process. So, for help, you turned to those you had learned to trust and/or those whose opinions you valued. Soon your view of yourself began to reflect their evaluations of what was positive and negative. These evaluations guided your behavior. "I am a bad boy for throwing rocks." "I'm a good girl for helping mother." "I was wrong to get angry, or cry, or get loud and boisterous." "I must not do that again." As you continued to grow, your self-concept continued this process of observing, evaluating, and selecting new experiences and responses. And once started in a certain direction it presumably continued in that direction.

The process is still going on. For example, you selected this book, supposedly because you thought it might have suggestions which would enable you to help young people grow. Fostering the growth of youth is a positive value consistent with your self-concept. You believe in your ability to help young people or you would not have bothered to consider organizing your future behavior in that direction. And, if I might be allowed to presume a bit further, I would speculate that your use of these exercises will depend to some extent on how secure you are about your sexual identity. These exercises present the possibility for each person to define their own sex-role identity; inclusive, exclusive, or overlapping with what has been traditionally considered "masculine" or "feminine" by external standards.

Let's return to the young people you work with. How can sexual stereotyping interfere with their development of a rich and positive self-concept?

It happens because young people's self-concept is strongly influenced by their sex-role identity. They decide what kinds of behaviors and options are possible for them on the basis of their sex-role identity. If they view themselves possessing dreams, characteristics, or behaviors they have learned are more appropriate to the opposite sex, the possibility of self-rejection and/or repression of characteristics of self increases. This publication is aimed at helping young people understand that everyone possesses so-called masculine and feminine characteristics to some extent, and that their energies, which are badly needed for growth and development, are not diverted into defending against or conforming to unnecessarily rigid definitions of masculinity and feminity. Maslow's supports this statement by describing his self actualizing subjects as having reached full humanness, and freedom from arbitrary sexual, cultural, and racial boundaries concerning what they could be.

A young persons sex-role identity is developed primarily in the home where parents provide major role models. If a father restricts himself to the "masculine chores" of the yard, tool chest and garage, his son is not likely to feel that washing dishes and cooking are masculine chores. And, if the mother is exclusively engaged in the domestic activities of cleaning, cooking and caring for others, her daughter may question whether women are to have other interests. Sexual identity is further set by the toys, clothes and room decor made available to boys and girls. Last, but not least, television advertising, programming, and the printed page provide very narrow sex-role definitions which further stamp in the cultural norms of what is "masculine" and "feminine".

It is not surprising, therefore, that a 1962 longitudinal study reported by Kagan and Moss[1] concluded that the differential effects of parental behavior on boys and girls, and the young person's own desire to make his/her behavior agree with the culture's definition of sex-roles, is a major factor determining the stability of male and female behavior over time. It is surprising how early boys and girls begin to learn the traditional behaviors considered appropriate to each sex and how readily they accept these as correct guides for their behavior, bringing pressure to bear on peers who deviate. Fagot (1977)[2] reports definite sex preferred behaviors among three and four year olds attending nursery school and that the sex-typing of activities had not changed much from 1968 to 1976. She further points out that boys who tried out opposite-sex preferred behaviors had fairly negative consequences in terms of peer rejection, and girls who did likewise received some negative feedback from their teachers and no positive reinforcement from their peers. At worst, they were ignored.

Negative consequences of sex-role experimentation is evident throughout childrens' school careers. The majority of students bring their behavior into conformance with the traditional cultural prescriptions of what is "feminine" and "masculine". One finds very few girls in sheet metal classes or electronics and few boys in the secretarial-type courses—except typing.

This process of bringing behavior into conformance with the expectation of others is not unrelated to what we ourselves have done. We know it most vividly in the spotlight and crises situations of our lives. As we experienced these spotlights and crises situations we also experienced a fairly good understanding of what the others about us expected our reactions to be. We might have given others a bit of what they expected from us even if it wasn't the same as our true feelings.

Behaving according to an image of what we think we ought to be can be necessary at times. The difficulty is that if we do much of this, we risk losing ourselves, our uniqueness and our potential. For example, the degrees of freedom are lessened for the girl who says and believes that being a pilot is a job best done by a man. She will never dream of herself as a pilot and consequently never engage in the exploratory activities which might have led her to find out otherwise.

This is what happens when young people conform to the expectancies as they influence the world of work. Their dreaming and exploration is reduced drastically. Studies of sex-stereotyping of occupations among elementary age students reveal that, even at this young age, the majority of them already stereotype occupations.

We have even fewer degrees of freedom if we engage in the process of being what others want us to be when the conforming behavior is out of our conscious control. That is, we are victims to our lack of awareness. This is best illustrated through adult expectancies that one sex or the other possess personality characteristics traditionally ascribed as "masculine" or "feminine". A dramatic example of this was reported recently in a study by Condry and Condry, (1976).[3] Adults were asked to label the emotions shown by a child in a series of filmed incidents. Half the adults believed the child to be a male while the other half believed the child to be a female. Emotions were labeled significantly different on the same behavioral incidents depending upon whether the labler believed him/her-self to be watching a girl or a boy. Boys, of course, were seen as significantly aggressive; and girls? You guessed it—fearful.

It is not hard to imagine how consistent day to day occurrences of this type can result in self-fulfilling prophecies for the young. "Oh, that frightened you didn't it, honey?" "You don't have to be afraid, I'll take care of you." "That made you angry didn't it, Son? Made you want to get back at em, eh?" Statements of this type compounded overtime can have the same effect on boys and girls that being told we don't look well five or six times in one day can have on us.

Adult expectations of this type can be especially devastating in a school setting where we know that boys generally need less aggressiveness and more impulse control to facilitate intellectual performance while girls need greater aggressivity and less inhibition to facilitate intellectual achievement. (Maccoby, Sutton, Smith, Roberts and Rosenberg, 1964,[4] Kagan and Moss, 1962[5])

Educators, and others helping youth to grow, need a chance to examine their own gender expectancies. In-service training exercises have been included in the last section of this book for this purpose. Included also are exercises which invite professionals to examine their practices concerning differential treatment of the sexes. All exercises are structured so that participants engage in planning future behavior from the insights they have gained.

The following assumptions underline the exercises designed for adults and students at each developmental level:

1. Each participant, regardless of age, is provided the means to assess and increase awareness of his/her attitudes and beliefs.
2. Each participant is asked to explore the etiology and implications of their attitudes and beliefs on their own and other people's future functioning.
3. Each participant is presented with situations for planning future experiences.
4. Each participant is encouraged to make his/her own self definitions and choices without shame or force.

In addition to the objectives of each exercise to eliminate sex stereotyping, the exercises for students include additional objectives in mental health, science literature, occupations, family life, dating, and education.

Why is there such contentiousness about helping students to define their sex-roles broadly? There is a major source of the disagreement on this question which seems to spring from the belief that a student learning of appropriate behaviors based on sex-role identification facilitates making same sex identification. Without same, there will be sex-role confusion leading to homosexuality, and lesbianism. This anxiety on the part of many adults merits factual answers and tolerance. Further, it indicates a need to teach sex differences and their relationship to the total self. For this reason, some exercises are presented in this book which might traditionally be termed "sex-education." These exercises are intended to supplement more formal sex-education programs. Appropriate cautions are presented along with these exercises and professionals are encouraged to work with others in the community who are involved in sex-education projects. When we are exposed to areas where sex-typed labels are arbitrary, we are better able to deal with the real differences.

It is helpful for professions to have information about the development of same sex identification which they can use and share with parents. This information is presented in more detail in the section dealing with the early years because a child's sex-identification·is completed by age five; a developmental milestone that involuntarily occurs around this age. No one can say with certainty how same-sex or crossed-sex identification takes place, but we can be sure that exercises, such as those contained in this book to broaden sex-roles do not interfere with this process. It is beneficial to recognize that nothing is to be gained by perpetrating rigid sex-role stereotyping in schools and public institutions.

Young persons must be allowed the opportunity to develop and achieve their full potential. They should feel free to express a full range of human emotions, physical activities, games, toys and books—all of them freed from sex-role stereotypes. What children in school and other institutions require most is individual differentiation not gender differentiation. To persist in differential treatment of the sexes only denies to one sex the advantages permitted to the other.

References

1. Kagan, Jerome and Moss, Howard. *Birth to Maturity*, New York, Wiley, 1962.

2. Fagot, Beverly I. "Consequences of Moderate Cross Gender Behavior in Preschool Children." *Child Development*, 1977, 48, 902-907.

3. Condry, John and Condry, Sandra. "Sex Differences: A Study of the Eye of the Beholder." *Child Development*, 1976, 47, 812-819.

4. Maccoby, Eleanor. "Woman's Intellect" in S. M. Farber and R. H. L. Wilson (Eds.), *Potential of Women*, New York; McGraw-Hill, 1963.

   Sutton-Smith, B. Roberts, J. W. and Rosenberg, B. G. "Sibling Associations and Role Involvement." Merrill-Palmer Quarterly, 1964, 10, 25-38.

5. op cit. Kagan and Moss, 1962.

The Early Years: Pre-Kindergarten Through Primary

The activities and exercises in this section are intended for use with children in pre-kindergarten (age 4) through the primary grades. The teacher will want to select and adapt those most appropriate to the needs of the particular group. The following discussion is presented to aid in this process.

The first six exercises in section 1, the Early Years, focus on the child's picture of him/herself as it relates to sex-role identity. The purpose of the exercises is to help boys and girls acquire a positive picture of self regardless of gender. Girls and boys are helped to see they have courage and fears and that these are human attributes. These exercises are specifically intended to help children develop self awareness and pride in their attributes and accomplishments; one ability found to distinguish highly competent six-year olds from those who have difficulty coping with day to day tasks (White, et. al., 1973).[1]

Exercise One, Two and Three assess the extent to which children stereotype certain personality characteristics such as aggressor, protector, helpless one. In addition, they provide modes of interventions. Children are encouraged to examine these human characteristics in themselves, those about them, in the literature, and the media, summarizing their conclusions. Children learn to see people as possessing strengths and weaknesses regardless of sex and to value the individual's broad experiencing of all emotions.

The purpose of Exercise Five; "To Be or What to Be" is for each child to focus on the values he/she and others ascribe to a person solely on the basis of gender and to redefine their thinking in line with the insights they achieve. This experience is particularly important to primary aged children because they are exposed more frequently to the birth event through the birth of siblings or other close ties in the family and neighborhood. They hear expression of preference for a boy or girl, from adults and they are more vulnerable to accepting adult evaluations than they will be later on.

In an article in the latest bulletin of the Population Reference Bureau, Dr. Nancy Williamson found after conducting survey studies on birth preferences of parents, that despite woman's liberation, a large majority of parents in the United States and nearly everywhere else would rather have boys than girls.

Dealing with the birth event and babies is the objective to Exercise Four; "Everybody's Fancy; Everybody's Fine." This exercise focuses specifically on how boys and girls differ in a positive emotional context and at an appropriate cognitive level. It is presented because such experiences are believed necessary for children to achieve sex-role clarity and because it is particularly in these early years that parents express concern about attempts to abandon sex-role typing. They want their children to have a self concept that includes viewing themselves as the particular sex — with sex role preferences, that match their biological sex, (same sex identification). "Fathers bathing children, and cooking; mothers going to work as road construction workers; no wonder Johnny is in the housekeeping corner again! With men and women interchanging roles how can the boy clearly understand what being masculine means?"

Johnny and Jane can understand what being masculine and feminine means. This means providing information and experiences that focus on the actual gender differences when a child can understand them — at his/her appropriate developmental level. A decision is required, however, as to whether the child-care center or school is the place to provide biological sex-education experiences. If that decision is affirmative, use exercises four, five and six to begin.

Sex education for young children is an increasingly controversial area and a great deal of preparation should take place to insure that the adults are comfortable with the subject and that they possess accurate information and the support and knowledge of the adults at home.

Developmental Information

It will be useful for the adult leading exercises in the Early Years to know that, by age two, most children have the ability to identify and label the different sexes, regardless of clothing or hair style. By age two and a half, almost all children are aware of their own sex category but the fact that they know what sex they are still does not guide their preference for activities and objects to any significant degree. It is not until age three, when all these previous learnings are assimilated, that the child begins to make choices and express preferences because of them, (Thompson, 1975).[2] We can, then, for our purposes, assume that the children in this age bracket are not confused about what sex they are. Our concern would be more appropriately geared to ensuring that they have positive feelings about this information. Positive feelings should provide a better milieu for the growth of like sex identification than negative ones.

The most up-to-date research on children's concepts of how people get babies (Bernstein and Cowan, 1975)[3] tells us that children's concepts follow a Piagetian developmental sequence and that sex information is not just taken in by children, no matter how carefully taught, it is assimilated or transformed at the child's present cognitive level. An illustration of these cognitive levels is given below as a guide. The average child at three-and-a-half years of age is at zero; that is he/she lacks comprehension. Thereafter, children move in sequence through the stages,

13

with the average child at stage four being almost nine years of age. It is important for the adult also to know that a child has difficulty understanding new information presented at more than one stage level above his/her own present level of development.

STAGE LEVEL	DESCRIPTION	ILLUSTRATION
Level 1 Children do not see a need for a cause of babies	Most 3-4 year olds believe that a baby has always existed but they have several different notions concerning how it comes to be in the mother's body. Some believe it was always there, others assume it was located somewhere else in the same form and then somehow came into the mother, and still others speculate about a series of transformations.	(How did the baby happen to be in your Mom's tummy?) It just grows inside. (How did it get there?) It's there all the time. Mommy doesn't have to do anything. She waits until she feels it. (You said the baby wasn't in there when you were there.) Yeah, then he was in another place in America. (In America?) Yeah, in somebody elses tummy. (In somebody else's tummy?) Yeah, and then he went through somebody else's vagina, then he went in, um, my Mommy's tummy. (In whose tummy was he before?) Um, I don't know who his, her name is. It's a her.
Level 2 Causes are assimilated from notions of people as manufacturers	Many children at the 4-6 year ages attribute babies to some cause; primarily to a person or persons who function as manufacturers, and a few children connect a father with the birth pro-	Maybe they just paint the right bones . . . Maybe they just paint the bones and paint the blood and paint the blue blood.

cess but transform what they have been told to a mechanical process.

Level 3		
Isolate social, biological, and sexual relationships but do not coordinate them	Many children at the 5-9 age level appear to have isolated three major ingredients in the creation of babies: social relations, external mechanics of sexual intercourse, and the fusion of biological genetic materials.	It's like when people are naked, and they're together, and they're together, and they just lie together, I guess. Like they're hugging. Some men give hickies, except my Dad don't. They're just together (What does that have to do with getting babies?) I don't know. I guess it's like mothers and fathers are related, and their loving each other forms a baby, I guess. (How?) I don't know. It's just there's love and I guess it forms a baby, like I said before.

In summary, Exercises One through Six provide the children with experiences which help them acquire self-concepts free from negative values and perceptions based on gender. They also provide a way for children to view themselves in the possession of a wide variety of human attributes. The exercises from Seven through Eleven focus less on facilitating pride in individual attributes. Instead, they spotlight objectives which deal with their opportunities to engage in all types of activities and accomplishments.

Exercise Seven provides an opportunity for children to learn they can solve their problems without excessive dependency. Exercise Eight focuses on the need for equality of rewards. This reinforces the theory of equal pay for equal work.

Kagan and Ender (1975)[4] postulate that one of the reasons why lower socio-economic children are often less achievement motivated is that parents of low socio-economic background are less likely to recognize "non-traditional" sex-roles. Exercise Eight can be expanded for use with the children in this category.

Exercises Nine and Ten put effort and preference together in the world of work. Dreaming about "What I want to be when I grow up," and "trying on roles," is one of the ways children expand their potentialities. Children need to be allowed to dream of themselves in many roles during the early years. Such fantasizing is essential in order for them to maximize later choices such as subject selection period, vocational — technical programs and college majors. We need not be concerned that this early fantasizing minimizes reality. Choices will narrow throughout the elementary and secondary school years as children learn more about themselves, the world of work and the requirements of particular occupations. The key concept *is not* to fall into the trap vocational theorists present when they discount children's early view of the world of work as romantic and unrealistic— it is, rather, to capitalize on this by presenting all occupations in as exciting and worthwhile light as possible.

Exercise Nine provides the means for introducing children to occupations. It allows the teacher to see what occupations are interesting to children; what occupations need to be made more interesting; and what occupations sex stereotype. It is particularly helpful for the adult to see where "internal bars" exist which could interfere with the childs exploring an occupation. The "internal bars" concept is best illustrated by girls responses on the "When I Grow Up Maybe I'll Be—" sheets provided in Exercise Nine. For example, many girls state they would like to be a pilot by circling the happy face but designate it a job for men by circling the male stick figure. Such bars can tip the scale towards a girl choosing the lower paid career direction of stewardess or reservation clerk, rather than the higher paid and more prestigious occupation of pilot. Girls are not electing courses in electronics, metal working, higher mathematics, and other traditionally male courses in secondary school even though these are now being opened up to them. It would seem that the "inner-bars" acquired from our culture in their early years have taught them that these fields are "un-feminine."

Exercise Ten provides a means for children to try-on occupational roles and to develop an interest in finding out more about them. It relies heavily on the use of imaginative play.

Exercise Eleven also focuses on play. By analyzing their everyday playthings and experimenting with adult reactions when they depart from the traditionally male or female toys, children can acquire some understanding of how they are influenced by adults to take on traditional roles in play and how this same influence affects their own feelings if they depart from these roles. The aim of this exercise is to free children in their play to respond to their own internal motivation and to manage adult reactions in constructive fashion.

References

1. White, Burton, L.; Watts, Jean C. *Experience and Environment: Major Influences on the Development of the Young Child.* Prentice Hall Inc., Englewood Cliffs, New Jersey, 1973.

2. Thompson, Spencer K. "Gender Labels and Early Sex Role Development." *Child Development*, 1975, 46, 339-347.

3. Bernstein, Anne C., and Cowan, Philip A. "Children's Concepts Of How People Get Babies." *Child Development*, 1975, 46, 77-91.

4. Kagan, Spencer, and Ender, Philip B. "Maternal Response to Success and Failure of Anglo-American, Mexican-American, and Mexican Children. *Child Development*, 1975, 46, 452-458.

Self-Enhancing Prophecy

Objectives For Children:
1. To describe children's expectancies regarding positive behavior traits on the basis of gender alone.
2. To compare children's expectancies with those of others.
3. To test reality sex-typed expectancies of positive behavioral traits through problem solving, discussion and analysis of stories.

For Teachers:
1. To assess the existence of children's sex-typed attitudes regarding positive behavioral traits.

Time Required:
Two, twenty minute blocks with a break between of one hour or less.

Number Of Participants:
25 maximum

Materials:
1. A teacher set of six 8½ x 11″ stick figure drawings to depict the six positive behavioral traits.
2. A teacher set of six behavioral descriptions to accompany the drawings.
3. Child answer cards, six times the number of children participating; and one crayon for each participant. (See end of exercise)
4. Sheets of newsprint, headed in advance, to record results with children.

Process:
1. The teacher will say to the class:
   "I am going to show you some pictures. Each picture shows a child doing something that this child does a lot. Look at the picture and decide whether that person is more likely to be a boy, a girl, or either."
2. The teacher shows the first picture, "Big Courageous", but does not give the picture that name aloud. The teacher reads the behavioral description that accompanies the picture.
3. Each child receives an answer card and is instructed to whether he/she thinks the person described sounds most like a boy, a girl, or either one. The cards are collected and labeled appropriately to distinguish them from each of the other five sets.
4. The teacher does the remaining five behavior descriptions in the same way; first, showing the picture without naming it and then reading the description. Students responses are collected. Encourage children to save comments for a later discussion.
5. The children's answer card data is analyzed by letting them assist in the counting and recording on newsprint. Mark the number of boy responses, number of girl responses, and number where both were indicated.
6. The teacher leads a discussion with the children helping them compare their answers with real behaviors they have observed. Children are encouraged to think about the origin of their sex-typed attitudes.
7. The teacher reads the book, *Blueberries for Sale* by Robert McCloskey, published by Viking Press. Children are asked if "Sal" acts like a boy or a girl, and asked how can they tell. Children are then encouraged to discuss whether activities should be limited to girls or boys only.
8. Children are asked to observe for one week to see if they or their friends encounter situations which limit activities to boys only or girls only. During the week a list is made of these incidents and activities limited to boys or to girls only are then discussed.
9. The teacher posts six different newsprint sheets with the titles: Courageous, Hard working, Friendly, Thinker, Honest and Protector. Children

are asked to watch for persons who behave like the descriptions. Write the names of these persons on the charts. This can be continued as long as there's interest.

Child Answer Card

SIX BEHAVIORAL DESCRIPTIONS

Big Courageous

This person is hardly ever afraid to try new things. This person goes to places like the dentist's office or birthday parties and knows what to do without worrying about strangers or acting shy and frightened. This person usually doesn't cry about falling down or getting shots either.

Hard Worker

This person will always do the work and even help do work for others. This person doesn't give up easily or say, "I can't". You can count on this person to put toys away, clean up, do school work and run errands.

Big Friendly

This person cares about other people. If you fall down or get hurt, this person will try to help. If you are sad, this person tries to cheer you up. This person always says Hi; usually shares and likes to play with other people.

Big Thinker

This person is very smart. This person usually can give the answers or tries to figure them out. This person almost always wants to know how come something works, or how come something is true. This person usually has a lot of good ideas about what to do or what to make.

Very Honest

This person does not try to pretend to be somebody special when they are not.

This person usually tells the truth even if it means getting in trouble for something done wrong.

Big Protector

You can count on this person to stand up for what is right and fair without being mean. This person can stop you from taking toys and things without hitting. This person takes care of own property, pets, family and friends without always getting into fights but still nobody pushed this person around.

Big Courageous

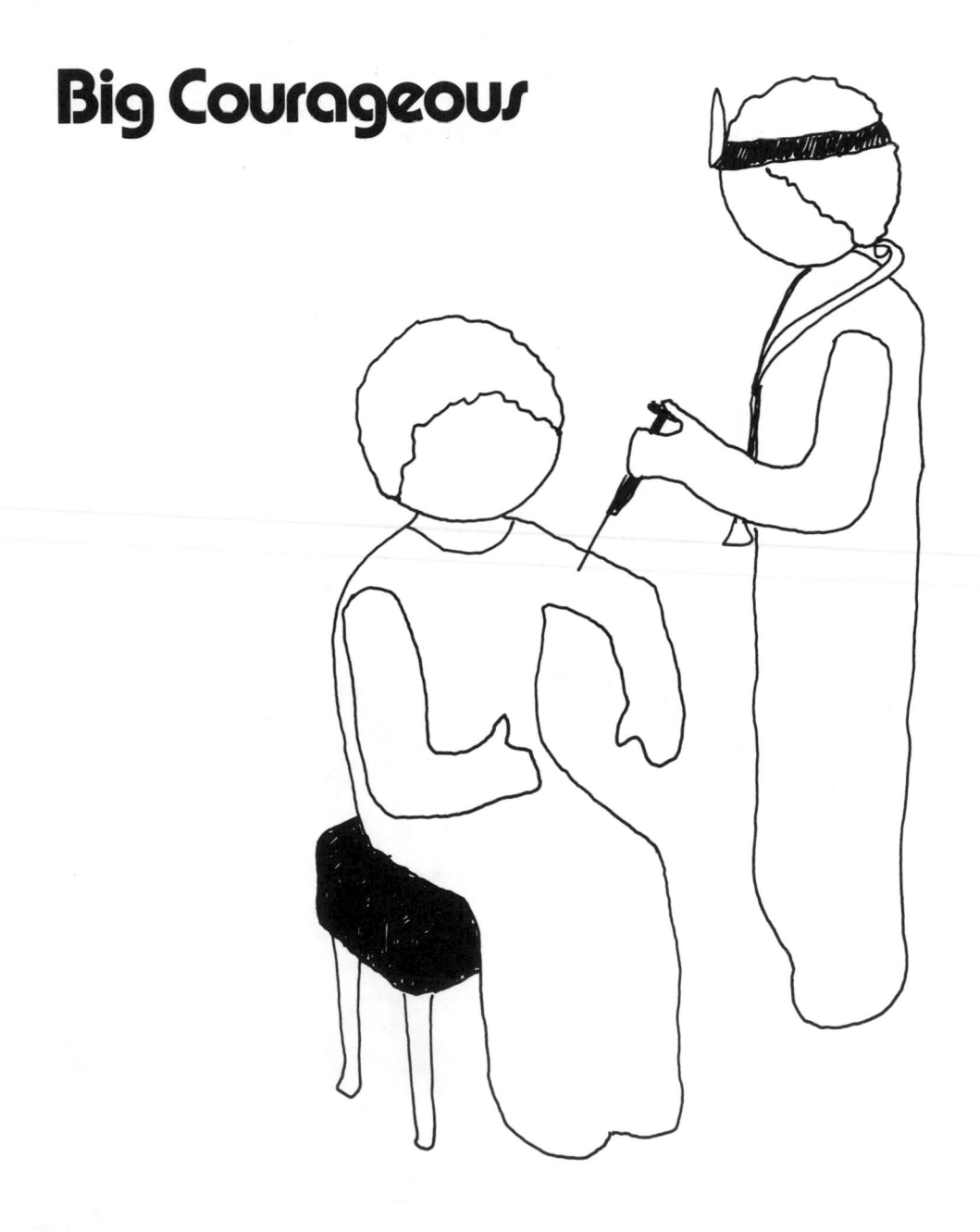

Hard Worker

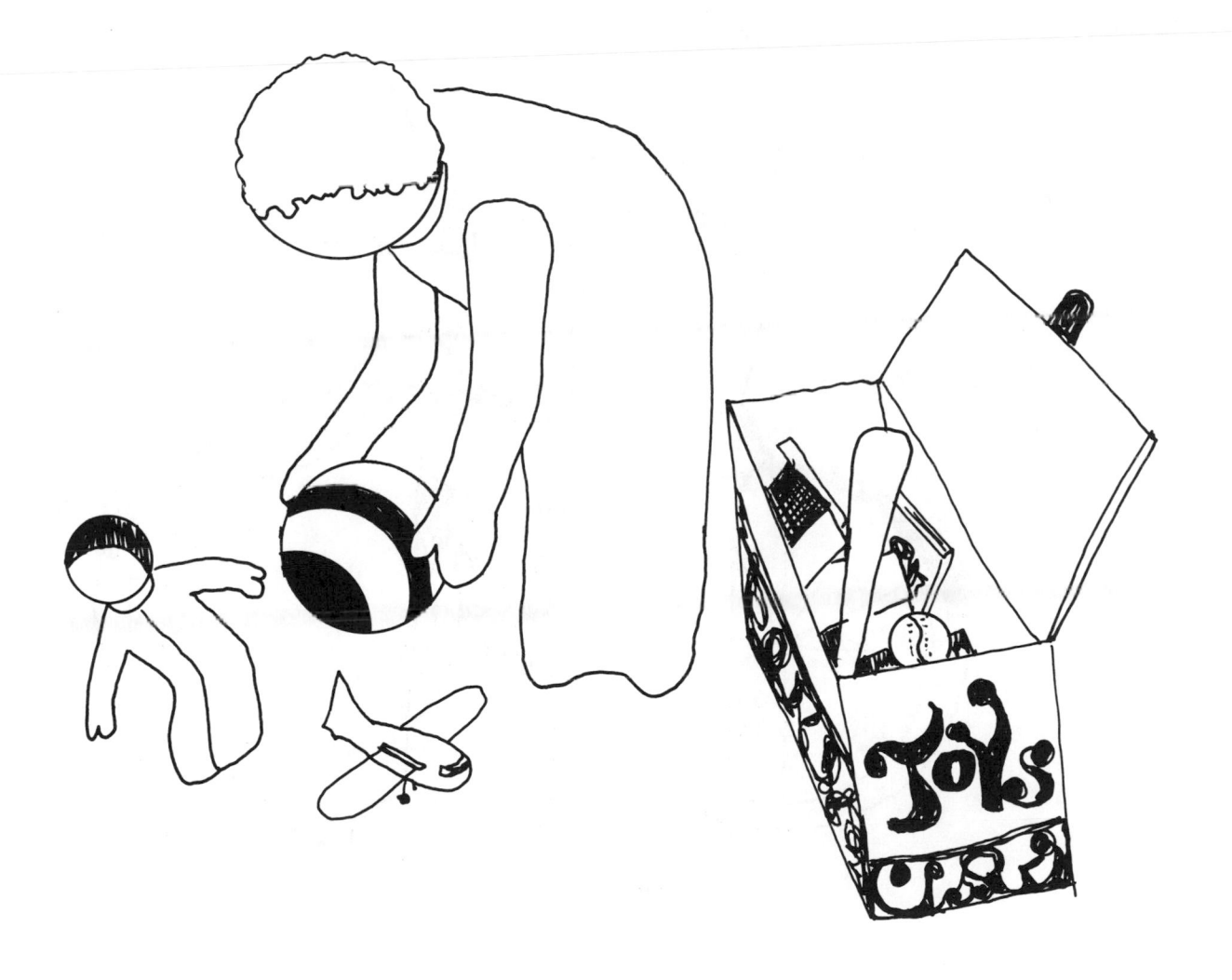

Big Friendly

Big Thinker

Very Honest

Big Protector

What You See Is What You Get

Objectives For Children:
1. To describe children's expectancies for negative behavior traits on the basis of gender.
2. To compare sex-typed expectancies for negative behavior.
3. To test the reality of these sex-typed expectancies through problem solving discussion and analyses of stories.

For Teachers:
1. To assess the existence of children's sex-typed attitudes about behavioral traits which are usually perceived as negative in mixed-sex-group interactions in the classroom.

Time Required:
Minimum of two separate 30 minutes time blocks

Number Of Participants:
25 maximum

Materials:

1. One teacher set of six 8½ x 11″ stick figure drawings which depict the negative behavior traits.
2. A teacher set of six behavior descriptions which accompany the above drawings.
3. Children's answer cards — six times the number of children and a crayon for each child.
4. Sheets of newsprint, headed in advance, on which to record data results and analyses.

Process:

1. The teacher will say to the class:
   "I am going to show you some pictures." Each picture shows a child doing something that the child does a lot. Look at each picture and decide whether that person is most like a boy, a girl or either one.
2. The teacher shows the first picture — "Big Fearful" — without using that name aloud and reads the behavioral description that accompanies the picture.
3. Each child is given an answer card and instructed to draw a circle around the person they think it is most like on the card. If they think it is like both, draw a circle around both. The teacher collects and labels this set of cards, "Big Fearful."
4. The teacher will do the remaining five behavior descriptions in the same fashion. Children are encouraged to save comments for a discussion later.
5. The teacher analyzes data with the class by letting children assist in the counting and recording on newsprint.
6. The teacher leads a discussion with the children which helps them compare their answers with behaviors they have observed. They are encouraged to think about where stereotyped attitudes come from. (T. V., movies, stories, etc.) Since this exercise deals with negative traits the teacher will want to be careful that no specific names of children in the class are identified with a particular description.
7. The teacher reads or tells the children the story of Chicken Little (Henny-Penny) and The Hare That Ran Away.* The children are asked to note the difference in sex between the two main characters. (These are in fact the same story with the main character differing in sex only.)
8. The children are told that in the subsequent days they will be read (or told) stories which have characters like each of the stick pictures. Children are asked to help find stories that have male and female characters for each stick picture.

Eastern Stories and Legends by M. Shedlock; E. P. Dutton, 1920.

SIX BEHAVIORAL DESCRIPTIONS

Big Fearful

This person is almost always afraid of something. Sometimes this person is afraid of things which will probably never happen. Other times this person is afraid or worried and doesn't even know what about.

Big Show-Off

This person seems to always want everyone's attention. This person will often do silly or exaggerated things to get people to notice. This person acts like this a lot but especially when visitors come or when this person is out before a lot of people.

Big Tattle-Tale

This person always watches other children. And when they do or say something wrong, this person says: "I'm going to tell on you." Lots of the time this person does tell too.

Big Do Nothing

This person usually doesn't want to do anything like play with others or learn and see new things. Almost all the time this person plays alone or just watches others.

Big Fighter

This person likes to show everyone how tough they are. If this person doesn't get what they want other people are likely to get hit or yelled at. This person can also throw rocks or call names.

Big Liar

This person makes up stories to make you believe they have everything the best or biggest. This person also lies when someone finds out they made a mistake or did a wrong thing.

Big Fearful

Big Show-Off

Big Tattle-Tale

Big Do Nothing

Big Fighter

Big Liar

Or Would You Rather Swing On A Star?

Objectives For Children:

1. To describe and increase children's awareness of their preference for certain personal characteristics.
2. To compare children's preferences to those of others and develop tolerance for individual differences.
3. To encourage children to try on (expand) their repertoire of personal characteristics.
4. To analyze data for preference patterns by sex and problem solve the reasons for any patterns found.

For Teacher:

1. To acquire knowledge of student understandings and preferences for personal characteristics which will aid in curriculum planning; e.g., individual children.
2. To assess growth in repertoire of personal characteristics for individual children.

Time Required:

Initial activity, steps through six take approximately 90 minutes in 2 separate fine blocks. Follow up activities continued only while interest is maintained.

Number Of Class Participants:
25 maximum

Materials:
1. Animal preference inventory; one copy for each child, (pages 40 - 42 and a crayon or pencil for each.
2. Teacher set of ten animal pictures (Bear, bird, butterfly, cat, elephant, lion, rabbit, shark, duck, wolf).
3. Newsprint, magic marker.

Author's Note:
Curious George was being read to a Kindergarten boy when half way through the story, he turned to his special adult and said: "I wish I was a monkey like George!" He expressed this wish several times for he knew somehow that the adult had no real sympathy for it nor understanding of its depth.

Most children at this age have occasions when they want to be animals. Not only are they a fascinating part of their world, but identification with animals provides a brief recess from the heavy pressures on the child to become more mature. Storytellers and authors have capitalized on this fact for generations and so can you if in meeting the following objectives.

Process:
1. The teacher will give each child a copy of the animal preference inventory; making sure also that seating prevents children looking on another's paper. The teacher will say:

   "We are going to pretend that we can be any or all the animals that we want for a little while. You will have to look at each animal as I say its name and decide if you would like to be that animal.

   "Find the first animal on the first page; it's a bear. Now put your finger on the happy face. Decide if you would like to be a bear but don't tell anyone your answer. If you would like to be a bear, circle the happy face. If you would not like to be a bear, ever, color the "I would not like face" the one where the mouth goes down like this (demonstrate). If you are not sure whether it would be fun to pretend to be a bear color the face in the middle."

2. The teacher will do each of the nine remaining animals in the same way.

The teacher will collect the papers; telling children they will discuss their choices later; and ask the children to move into the center of a large circular or square area around which are posted the pictures of the same ten animals that were on the inventory. This time the teacher will instruct the children to look carefully at the pictures and decide which animal that they would most like to be of all ten. Encourage each child to make a choice of his/her own. Then go stand (by/under) the animal of his/her choice.

3. With the children sitting in these ten clustered areas, let each child explain why he or she would most like to be that animal. Let them show why with pantomime if they like. Question, if necessary to determine what it is about the animal that the child prefers.

4. Call on pairs of children to demonstrate through brief dramatizations what might happen if the two animals got together (in center of circle). For example — a duck and shark. The key theme here is fun and creativity with children allowed to try on roles that they believe these animals typify. For example, aggressor, shy person.

END OF FIRST BLOCK OF TIME

5. With the children now in possession of their animal preference inventory, analyze the following data:

   a. Use a separate newsprint sheet for each animal. Ask "how many would like to be a bear?" Count hands and record data on newsprint.

   EXAMPLE: Bear

BOYS	GIRLS	BOYS AND GIRLS

   b. Since most stories of animals have males as main characters, try to match two stories which portray the same animal as having opposite personality characteristics. Example:

   Chicken Little — a female who is foolish and overly fearful

   Crocodile and Hen — female hen is wise and doesn't show fear

6. *Dramatizations* — After reading animal stories, let children identify the number of characters. Write their names on a slip and let children draw a part to play regardless of sex. Assign roles on basis of experimenting with personal characteristics. For example, who hasn't had much of a chance to act naughty lately? (and would like to) Or let all the girls play all the parts one time and then all the boys the next and contrast by children's observations from watching and by children's comments of how it feels to try certain roles like the big bad wolf.

7. Let children compare their impressions of males and females of each specie of animals against factual information about the male and female of each species.

BEAR

BIRD

BUTTERFLY

CAT

ELEPHANT

RABBIT

LION

SHARK

DUCK

WOLF

Everybody's Fancy; Everybody's Fine

Objectives For Children:
1. To develop children's increased self awareness of their bodies.
2. To develop a more positive body image relative to gender.
3. To develop a greater sense of group caring and tolerance.
4. To discriminate the essential physical features of sex difference.
5. To describe and compare values of privacy in a factual, low anxiety atmosphere.

Time Required:
Minimum 1 hour

Number Of Class Participants:
Maximum of 25 with teacher (Assistance from a volunteer parent, nurse or physician can enhance activity.)

Materials:
1. Anatomically realistic dolls or appropriate visual aids supplied by the medical profession.

a. Hand-Sewn Anatomically Realistic Dolls are made to order in any U.S. minority from Children's Music Center, 5373 West Pico, Los Angeles, California 90019 ($22)
b. L'il David and L'il Ruthie are made with true-to-life features in black or white vinyl (boy in blue romper, girl in pink).
c. "Mooks;" cloth dolls with anatomical detail hand embroidered faces in white or brown, and male and female. Erica Dodenhoff, 25 Bruceville Road, High Falls, N. Y. ($20)

Process:

This activity would follow children who have had some experiences with clay.

1. Tell the children that they will be doing a pretend activity where they will pretend to model a classmate from clay. Structure the activity by having them choose a partner.
2. The teacher then selects a child for demonstration purposes from one of the pairs.

   EXAMPLE:

   "Alicia, I am going to pretend to make you of clay. Let's see how many balls of clay I will need? One ball for the head, another large ball for the body and four more; rolled out a bit for the arms and legs. (Teacher pats with hands as each ball is imaginarily supplied and put in place pantomime fashion.) Now, I want to work very carefully on this fine head. First I'll smooth it to the proper shape; oval with this nice firm chin. Now I want to add on hair; long silky hair or short and marvelously curly; now for the ears. How many do I need? I must remember to shape them as delicately." Stop occasionally and ask the child how she/he feels about a particular feature.
3. Since this is an exercise in delineating the physical attributes and helping the individual build a well defined and positive body image, when the teacher feels the tone has been set and that the other children understand the activity, the children may begin. They may comment only on the features they like; telling why, and asking their partner how each one feels about each feature.
4. As the teacher moves about assisting in positive fashion, note when the pairs are confronting the problems of the genital area. (This is usually evidenced by avoidance and nonverbal communication—shy, awkward, embarrassed, fearful, giggling, and knowing looks.) The teacher stops the activity at this point.
5. The teacher, or a special adult, leads a discussion with all the class about their feelings of embarrassment. If the children are unable to verbalize at

first, the teacher should try to assist by labeling children's feelings. This will lead to a discussion of what children have been taught about privacy and how this relates to "what other children know."

6. The teacher, or special adult, then presents the appropriate biological names for the separate anatomical features of boys and girls by use of visual aids.

7. The discussion may be extended to clarify why some children act silly, embarrassed or curious. This helps children establish appropriate guidelines for responding to these situations.

8. Further extension of the discussion could deal with parental reactions and the reasons for same; culmination in a clarification of the value of privacy and establishment of guidelines for school and classroom. (Name calling, use of the bathroom, etc.)

9. The activity ends by allowing each child to tell one feature that he/she especially liked about the person they pretended to model of clay and one feature of their own that they especially like.

(Optional) You may want to introduce the song, *Everybody's Fancy, Everybody's Fine* by Fred Rogers (Mr. Rogers of T.V. fame).

EVERYBODY'S FANCY, EVERYBODY'S FINE

Some are fancy on the outside.
Some are fancy on the inside.

Everybody's fancy, everybody's fine.
Your body's fancy and so is mine.   Refrain

Refrain

Only girls can be the mommies.
Only boys can be the dads.

Refrain

I think you're a special person
And I like your in and outsides.

Refrain

To Be Or What To Be

Objectives For Children:
1. To increase children's awareness of their own sex.
2. To contrast children's ideas with those of others.
3. To analyze the bases upon which these ideas are determined.

Time Required:
Minimum of 20 minutes per group. Total class follow-up, 30 minutes.

Number Of Class Participants:
May be done in groups of 5 to 10 members, or individually

Materials:
1. Child Answer Card (two for each child)
2. Newsprint, magic marker
3. A large golden fish (optional)

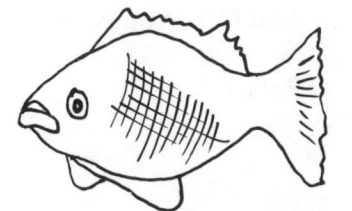

Process:

1. Tell the children that you are going to tell or read them a story, and that they will help make up the ending.

    An old fisherman and woman had lived together for many years. The only thing that made them sad was that they had never had any children to love and watch grow up. One day the old fisherman went out to catch fish without his wife. He was just about to give up when there was a tug on his line. The fisherman had caught a fish that was all golden in color. It was so beautiful that he didn't want it to die. He put the fish into a large tub and carried it home to show the fisherwoman. Imagine how surprised they were when the fish began to talk to them!

    "I am a magic fish and if you will throw me back into the sea, I will grant you three wishes."

    The fisherman and fisherwoman wished first for a child. Their second wish was to live long enough to help and watch the child grow up. The fish then told them that for their third wish they would have to tell whether they wanted a boy-child or a girl-child.

2. Each child is given an answer card and asked to finish the story by drawing a circle around the choice that the fisherman and woman should make. The teacher collects their answer cards, keeping boys and girls cards separate.

3. Without further discussion, the teacher asks each child to share the reason(s) why they chose as they did. As children give reasons, the teacher records them on Newsprint:*

<u>REASONS FOR CHOOSING BOY</u>   <u>REASONS FOR CHOOSING GIRL</u>

*In the three years that this question has been posed to groups of young children; cumulative data analysis reveals the following:

a. 82% of the boys respond boy while only 52% of the girls chose their own sex.

b. The reasons for sex choice are not significantly different regardless of whether a boy or girl answers. That is, boys and girls at a very early age share similarly learned stereotypic values ascribed to being male or female.

c. The reasons given by almost 80% of the boys fall in one or all of these three categories:

      boys are stronger
      boys can do more things
      boys grow up to work

d. The reasons given by almost 90% of the girls fall in one or all of these three categories:

      girls are prettier
      girls can have babies
      girls can do housework

4. Discussion: If all members of the class participate in several small group sessions, this major discussion can be done with the class as a whole.

   Re-read the story and ask the children to think about the reasons that were given for choosing boy or girl as you read them from the newsprint. If necessary, stimulate the discussion by asking: Are these reasons true? Are these the only reasons for choosing a girl or boy?

5. Tell the children the following information that you derived from counting their answer cards:

   "There are _____ boys in our class. _____ of the boys chose boy and _____ of the boys chose girl."

   "There are _____ girls in our class. _____ of the girls chose boys and _____ of the girls chose girl."

   Ask the children why they think these figures are what they are.

6. Plan an activity which allows the children to finish the story again in light of what they have just learned. This time sharing their reasons aloud with the whole class.

An `Eggsacting´ Responsibility

Objectives For Children:
1. To experience and clarify feelings involved in care-giver (parental) role; more specifically:
   a. accepting sex of child as predetermined
   b. preparing for a baby—place to sleep, clothes to wear
   c. accepting constant responsibility for baby's safety and security
2. To describe and compare learning outcomes; for example, is being a good caregiver dependent on your sex, traditions in dress, etc.

Time Required:
Each step varies depending upon the maturity of class: book activity is two day lesson plan.

Number Of Class Participants:
Maximum 30 children and 2 adults

Materials:
1. One egg for each participant. Color of egg should match ethnic composi-

tion of class.
2. Pink and Blue construction paper, with matching gift ribbon to make bonnets for "egg babies."
3. One milk carton to make a cradle for each egg child.
4. Scraps of material for lining cradle and making a blanket and pillow.
5. Equal number of boy and girl cards.
Total number will equal number of participants.
6. Newsprint and magic marker for experience charts.

Process:
First Day
1. Children are told they are going to do a pretend activity which will give them a little chance to see what it feels like to be a mother or a dad.

"We are going to pretend that your mother, aunt, neighbor, is going to have a baby and that very soon after you will be left in charge of taking care of the baby for one whole day while they are away."

"Now, of course, each of you cannot have a real live baby, so instead I am going to give you an egg."

2. Explain or determine through questioning why an egg is being used. Be sure that your children understand the similarity of the "fragileness" of an egg to a baby. Explain the difference between an egg and a baby; that is, babies do not come from eggs and a lost or damaged egg is not terribly serious. You decide soft boiling the eggs is a necessary step.
3. Tell the children that their homework for tonight is to think of a name for the baby. If a child comes with a prepared alternative for the baby regardless of sex, this is to be their own idea. Tell them only that the sex will be determined by drawing from a hat.

"This baby will be very special to you because you are going to be allowed to choose its name."

4. Let each child make a baby bed from the milk cartons and scraps. Individual differences in terms of elaborateness of preparation can be insured by allowing plenty of time and other activity choices in a freely structured situation.

Second Day:
5. Before the children arrive, place the appropriately colored egg in each child's bed. Be sure that the name of each child is clearly indicated on the bed they made. When the children arrive let them pass by the nursery to see that their "egg children" are waiting.

6. Each child draws the particular sex of his or her "egg" child from a hat. Allow ample time for *all* children to express and discuss their feelings regarding the sex of their "egg" baby. Have them share and relate these feelings expressed with what comments they have heard from friends and family when births are announced.

7. Give each child who has a "girl egg" a pink bonnet and give a "blue bonnet" to each "parent" of a "boy egg." Ask why they got the color they did. "Does it have to be this way? Why is it? What are you told you must wear because you are a girl or a boy?" Allow children to exchange bonnets if they desire, then ask each child to write the name of his/her "egg baby" on the bonnet. (Write it for those not able to do so.)

8. Let each child weigh and measure their egg, with assistance from the aide or volunteer. Record the heights and weights and announce to the class who has the biggest, smallest "baby." Let children verbalize their feelings about this.

9. Let each child know that they are responsible for their egg child the rest of the day and that they will not give them back to you until time to go home. (For older children or for classes where parents are cooperating, you may want to let the children keep the "babies" overnight and return them in the morning.)

> Throughout the day you will want to be alert to what is happening and available to handle feelings for a few eggs will be lost, misplaced temporarily, damaged, etc. A sobbing child with a broken egg can be given some other status responsibility for the day. Often children will offer to share. A child may even want to give his egg up for adoption and should be allowed to do so without guilt producing comments. There are an "eggsquisite" number of spontaneous possibilities for learning and if more than two aware and compassionate adults are available, it is useful.

10. During the day, record on previously posted newsprint behaviors and comments as they occur.

KEEPING AN EYE ON EGG BABIES

Boys do:

Boys say:

KEEPING AN EYE ON EGG BABIES

Girls do:

Girls say:

---

11. At the end of the second day or beginning of the third, if children have continued overnight, the children will return the eggs and there will be a reporting time for feelings about returning the eggs and for feelings and learnings about the entire activity. These will be written up as experience charts. Take special care to analyze the data secured in step eleven to see if there were similarities and differences between the boys and girls. Discuss reasons why or why not.

Questions which may be used to elicit summary learnings:
    a. What did we learn about getting ready for a baby?
    b. How did you feel about your egg baby? at first? after a few hours?
    c. How did you feel about giving the egg baby back?
    d. What do you think is the most difficult thing about egg babies? Do you think this is true of real babies?
    e. What do you think is the most enjoyable thing about caring for an egg baby? Do you think this is true about real babies?

Dependency

Objectives For Children:
1. To develop awareness and describe attitudes of dependency related to their own sex.
2. To analyze the reasons for allocating dependent and independent behaviors to one sex or the other.
3. To engage in problem solving situations and not who offers solutions while determining some of the factors upon which "good" problem solving depends.

Time Required:
Minimum of 30 minutes

Number Of Class Participants:
30

Materials:
1. A data analysis newsprint sheet prepared in advance and magic marker.
2. A sheet of drawing paper and crayons for each child or a casette tape

recorder for each child to dictate first his/her name and then problem solution.

3. A set of the three illustrations.

Example of Data Analysis Sheet

BOYS	GIRLS	
_____	_____	no solution
_____	_____	unreal or magic solution
_____	_____	a waiting for help solution (for example, children waited until help arrived)
_____	_____	a making help happen solution (e.g., children called for help)
_____	_____	a problem solving together solution
_____	_____	the boy solved the problem
_____	_____	the girl solved the problem

Process:

1. The teacher tells the children a story, and they are going to make up the ending.

"Two children, a boy and a girl, went on a picnic with their families. After eating the two children decided to take a walk and explore the woodsy area nearby. Their families told them to be sure to return at dark because they were going to build a fire and toast marshmallows. The children said they would for it was about an hour before dark. During their exploring trip they walked across a rotten old door which covered a deep hole. The rotten door broke and they dropped down into a deep hole. Luckily they were not hurt. But the top of the hole was just over their heads."

(See illustration at the end of this exercise.)

2. The teacher says, I want each of you to think of an ending for this story and

> "go one at a time to the _____ and tell your ending into the tape recorder."

or

> "draw a picture which you can show while you tell the rest of us your ending."

3. As children tell their story endings, the teacher can tally their solutions on the newsprint chart. (This step can be done by the teacher alone or with a small group if tape recorder is used.)

4. The teacher leads a discussion with the children giving consideration the following points: after the children have seen the tallies and at least hear one illustration of each category
   - Which kinds of solutions do you think are best and why?
   - Did only boys think boys could solve the problem? Why?
   - Did only girls think girls could solve this problem? Why?
   - What do we call solving a problem together? Can you tell us about some times when you have seen this happen?

5. The teacher divides the children into small groups of four or six with mixed sex composition. Give each group a problem to solve. Have each group report back later to the whole group about what took place when they tried to solve the problem.

6. Write up or discuss what took place touching upon the points in step four.

SAMPLE PROBLEMS TO SOLVE

1. A boy wants to play in the housekeeping corner, fixing meals and tending children. The other boys laugh at him and call him "weird". What should be done?

2. Jose's father drops him off to school everyday and kisses him good-by; the other kids start teasing him about this. What should Jose do?

3. Willie and Shirley like to play hospital but Willie refuses to play unless he can be the doctor. Shirley is tired of being the nurse and wants a chance to be the doctor. What should be done?

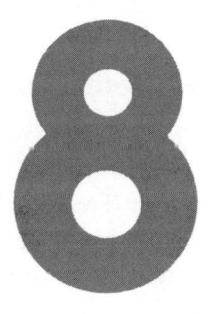

Deservedness

Objectives For Children:
1. To develop awareness of children's attitudes of "deservedness of reward" related to their own sex.
2. To identify the basis on which rewards are fairly given regardless of sex.
3. To resolve and describe a fair solution to a dilemma situation.

Time Required:
1 hour

Number Of Class Participants:
30

Materials:
1. Child answer cards, one for each child.
2. Newsprint
3. Magic markers

*Note: Prepare data analysis sheets for total group in advance.

Process:

The children are divided into small groups of 8-10. The teacher works separately with each group for step 2-4.

1. Tell the children that you are going to tell or read them a story, and that they will help make up the ending.

   "Two children, a boy and a girl, heard a TV announcement which said that for every 20 pounds of paper collected a free circus ticket would be given. There was only one more day before the circus. The two children decided to work together and collect papers from their homes and their neighbors. They both worked hard but they only collected 20 pounds to turn in. They only got one circus ticket thus making it possible for only one of them to go. Who should get the ticket?"

2. Each child is given an answer card and asked to finish the story by circling who gets the ticket. Ask them to save questions and comments for later. Collect the answer cards for the girls and boys separately.

3. The teacher leads a discussion around the circle letting each child tell his/her choice; stating the reason(s) for the choice without comment until all children have had their turn. The teacher records children's responses on newsprint in abbreviated fashion.

4. The teacher summarizes the data from each small group on large sheets of newsprint as follows.

   a. Answer cards

				None
Boy's choices				
Girl's choices				

   b. Tally the reasons beside the appropriate category regardless of the sex of the child responding. More than one response may be tallied for each child.

_____ no reason given

_____ a fairer solution should be found or was offered

_____ boy probably worked harder

_____ boys would like the circus more

_____ girl probably worked harder

_____ girl would like the circus more

_____ girl because it's polite; or because its unusual when
a girl does the same amount of work as a boy

_____ _____

_____ _____

---

5. The teacher presents the summarized data to the total group and initiates discussion by asking the children to note differences and similarities between the boys and girls choices and reflect aloud on the meaning of the patterns they find.

Children are asked to decide which of the reasons given is the fairest; or to supply a fairer solution. The teacher tries to get consensus on the fairest solution and have the children identify the basis on which a fair solution is arrived at.

Information For The Teacher:

A fundamental principal of Equity Theory states that a person will seek a division of rewards in which the rewards are proportional to the contribution or effort put forth. Research on reward allocation with 5 and 7 year olds who were asked to allocate rewards to others reveals that they do so largely on the basis of equity (Leventhal, Popp, and Sawyer, 1973) and that sex has no effect on reward allocation (Streater and Chertkoff, 1976).

The dilemma in the above activity is presented in such a way that it does not seem possible to allocate the reward equitably and therefore the children's answers are more likely to reveal bias such as:

a. Like sex choice tends to reveal self interest; e.g., I chose boy because I'm a boy or I chose girl because I'm a girl.

b. Cross sex choice tends to reveal sex-stereotypes; e.g., it's more polite to let girls have it.

c. Reasons which change the reality of the situation often reveal sex-stereo-typed attitudes; for example:

    change effort — boy worked harder

    change reward — get two tickets

Anything They Want To Be

Objectives For Children:
1. To identify job areas of interest.
2. To identify job areas which they sex stereotype.
3. To examine the validity of the basis upon which they sex-stereotype certain jobs.
4. To expand their knowledge about the world of work.
5. To be encouraged to choose activities which help them learn respect for all types of work.

Time Required:
1 hour

Number Of Class Participants:
Dependent upon maturity of group; small groups of 5-10 or total class.

Materials:
1. "When I Grow Up Maybe I'll Be—" one sheet for each child. Teacher will make ditto sheets for each child like the two samples provided from the

Developmental Inventory of Vocational Interest and Sex Role Appropriateness in Appendix A. Only one sheet is used each time the activity is done.

2. Newsprint, magic marker and a crayon for each child.

Process:

1. Before beginning, the teacher takes a few minutes to be sure that the children understand the concept of job as including the work a person does on a regular basis to earn money and/or give meaning to their lives. The teacher gives one or two illustrations of jobs that are not on the job sheet of the children. The teacher checks understanding by having children list some jobs they know.

2. Teacher says: "I am going to give you a sheet of paper which has one side folded back. Do not unfold it until I tell you to."

   "Look at the first job on this sheet. What do you think the job is?" (Pause for answers, then supply answer if need be.)

   "Let me read to you what a pilot does. The teacher reads the short description that accompanies the job, twice."

   "If you think that you might like to be a pilot when you grow up, color in the happy face to show that is a job you think you would be happy doing. If you think you would not be happy doing a pilot's job when you grow up, color the not happy face. If you aren't sure, color the face in the middle."

3. The teacher will check over the papers quickly to make sure all children understand and then go on to do exactly the same with the other five jobs on the sheet.

4. Now the teacher will say:

   "Unfold the last columns on this page. Once again I will read the description for each job and this time you will answer by marking in the last column. Let's start with item one, pilot (Read the job description again). Now look over at the last column. If you think this job could be done best by a man, circle the male stick figure. If you think this job could best be done by a woman, circle the female stick figure. If you think it could be done just as well by either a man or a woman, circle both stick figures at the bottom of the box."

5. The teacher will analyze and record the data from the children's job sheets with the children. Children can raise their hands whild the teacher counts and records on newsprint the following information:

EXAMPLE:

We Like These Jobs	Boys Can Do	Girls Can Do	Both Can Do
Pilot 𝍤𝍤𝍤 I ⑯	Pilot ㉓	Nurse ㉔	Sales Clerk ⑫
Barber/Hair Sytlist ⑫ 𝍤𝍤II	Sales Clerk ②	Sales Clerk ⑮	
Engineer III ③	Engineer ⑳		
Nurse 𝍤𝍤III ⑬			
Sales Clerk 𝍤𝍤 ⑩			

6. Teacher will lead a discussion with children about their job perceptions. The following questions should be helpful to guide the discussion:

- It looks like most people like the _____'s job; why is that?
- Not many people seem to like the _____'s job; why do you think? (The above questions will help the teacher decide how much information they have about particular jobs and the basis upon which students at this age express liking or disliking.)
- Why do you think so many of us thought that _____ was a man's job (woman's job)?
- Why can't both men and women do _____ job?
- What are some other things that people do in a _____ job?
- What jobs don't we know very much about?

7. The teacher will want to wind up the discussion by having children make up a new list by looking once again at the jobs and raising their hands only. The new lists on newsprint should be headed: JOBS WE WANT TO KNOW MORE ABOUT. JOBS THAT BOTH MEN AND WOMEN CAN DO.

8. Follow-up activities like those on the next page can be chosen if interest is maintained.

Follow-up Activities:
1. Role Try Out Boxes (See exercise 10)
2. Children can discuss work with people in non-stereotyped occupations; that is, a female physician, dentist, engineer or male nurse, secretary, etc. Have visitors tell about their work. Let children ask questions; discuss other people they know in non-stereotypical occupations; and share feelings about how they feel about men in typically female occupations

and about women in typically male occupations.

3. Ask children to count how many men and how many women they find shown on television in each of the jobs. Include Sesame Street and Mr. Rogers as a part of recommended viewing.

4. Games: Judy Floor Puzzles are two feet by three feet when assembled. The City, The Park, and Neighborhood Medical Clinic show multiracial male and female workers, kids and parents (Judy Co. $9.75).

5. Ask each child to ask some girl not in their class and one boy not in their class what they want to be when they grow up. Then ask them what they would want to be if they were the opposite sex. Each child will then report back to the whole class.

When I Grow Up Maybe I'll Be _____ .

1		PHYSICIAN — Doctors help make sick people well. They help people to stay well, too.		
2		FIREFIGHTER — A person who puts out fires and provides rescue services to people in the community.		
3		CHILD CARE WORKER — A person who works to help young pre-school children to learn and grow; at home, the nursery or anywhere.		

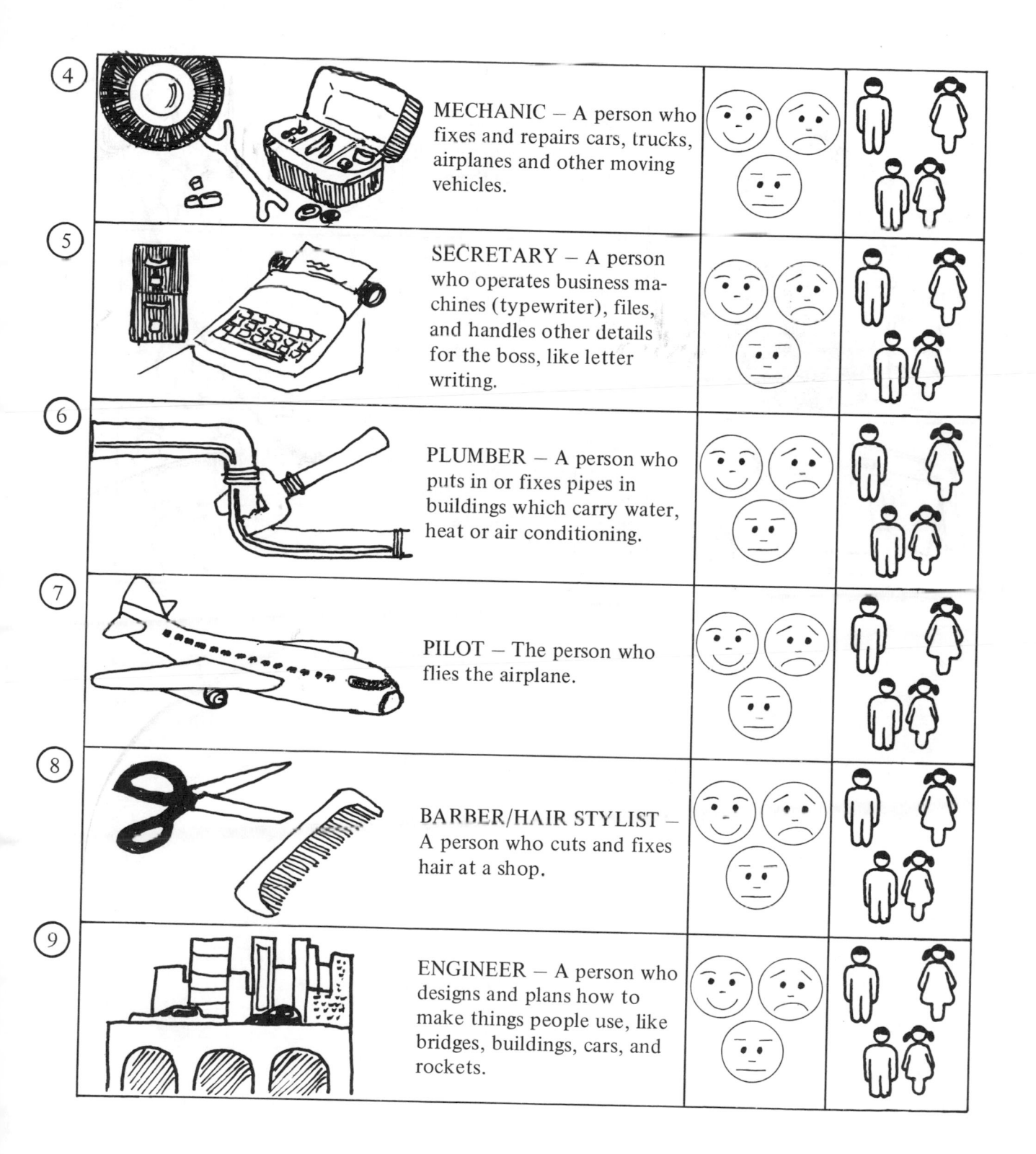

④ **MECHANIC** — A person who fixes and repairs cars, trucks, airplanes and other moving vehicles.

⑤ **SECRETARY** — A person who operates business machines (typewriter), files, and handles other details for the boss, like letter writing.

⑥ **PLUMBER** — A person who puts in or fixes pipes in buildings which carry water, heat or air conditioning.

⑦ **PILOT** — The person who flies the airplane.

⑧ **BARBER/HAIR STYLIST** — A person who cuts and fixes hair at a shop.

⑨ **ENGINEER** — A person who designs and plans how to make things people use, like bridges, buildings, cars, and rockets.

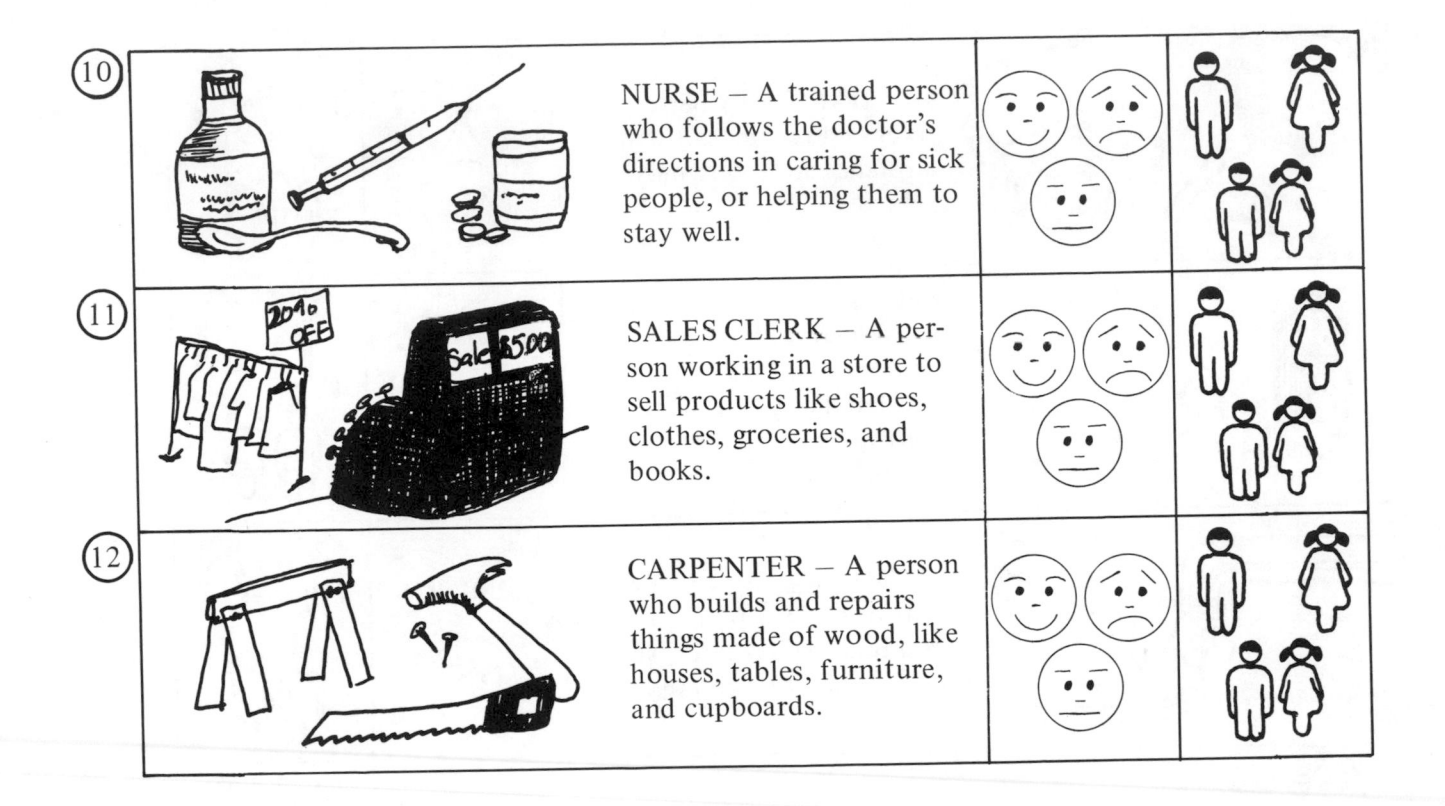

⑩ **NURSE** — A trained person who follows the doctor's directions in caring for sick people, or helping them to stay well.

⑪ **SALES CLERK** — A person working in a store to sell products like shoes, clothes, groceries, and books.

⑫ **CARPENTER** — A person who builds and repairs things made of wood, like houses, tables, furniture, and cupboards.

Role Try On Boxes

Objectives For Children:
1. To actively and creatively participate in trying on adult roles.
2. To expand children's perceptions to dream of future alternative work roles within their realm of possibility.
3. To receive an initial introduction to occupations in the world of work.
4. To remove inner bars of sex discrimination through changing perceptions of occupations as sex-related.

Time Required:
Minimum of 20 minutes for introducing each role try-on box

Number Of Class Participants:
Open

Materials:
1. One sturdy large sized shoe box or equivalent for each "role try-on".
2. Pictures of each sex utilizing tools of trade glued on boxes to aid in providing ideas for situations in which the occupational role may be tried on.

3. "Image makers": See sample list which follows for image makers associated with occupational role. For examples of further occupations, see Appendix A. If cooperative play is also an objective, include several image makers which are related to the occupational area; always remembering to introduce them so that neither sex is restricted from playing any role. For example, steward and stewardess, co-pilot and air controller could all be included in an airline box as could others. (The box would, of course, no longer be labeled pilot.)

4. "Tools of the trade": See list of image makers, tools of trade associated with each occupational role.

"Role Try-On Box" with contents.

Process:

1. The teacher tells children that today we are going to try on how it feels to be and work with a _____.

   Example: Today we are going to try on a pilot's job; a pilot who flies passengers to many different places in the world. Hold up a map on which pictoral symbols give clues to potential destinations, and include class in deciding where the pilot will be flying.

2. Ask for volunteers. Have the children do the "image makers."

   Example: Who would like to try-on being pilots? Here are the pilot hats. (Deal with difference between pilot and co-pilot and assigning of less important status role to one sex or other, consistently.) We'll just pretend you have on uniforms on which to pin these wings. Now we must choose names for our pilots and for the airline.

3. Facilitate the role playing situation through making up a story with your class or the participants. The story serves as a model for children's future use of the box by introducing the tools of trade and ways to use them! The story also provides encouragement for use of the imagination.

Example: Let us begin by having Pamela and Pete Pilot sitting in the cockpit of the passenger plane. These two chairs can be the pilots' seat and we'll set this instrument panel on the table before the chairs. How about it pilots, can you still look out and see the runway? Is it clear? (Calling another child's name) _____, will you be our control tower operator and tell us when the air above is clear for take off. OK, now pilots while you're waiting for that why don't you look over the instrument panel here and check everything out. Then you can check your route (etc. facilitating where needed with information).

Ready, now? Well, I guess we better tell the passengers, (indicating all the class) to fasten seat belts and whatever else you pilots do.

As flight ensues a storm can be imagined; sound effects provided by nonverbal students, and half the passengers show courage while half show panic. Only yours and the class imagination need limit the possibilities for the new airport in the classroom.

4. Close this introductory session by telling children that this box goes into the Competency Corner (a shelf where there are pigeon holes for many such boxes to be, and be added to). Encourage them to take out boxes in their free time activity. Also make a list of the questions that children now have about this occupation on paper and use this list for the planning of future field trips or visitors.

Alternate Example:

If there is not space for a Competency corner with role try-on boxes, you may want to consider using a puppet stage or a table top stage with cut outs used in the same fashion. (See top of next page.)

"Puppets"

"Cutouts"

Sample List of Occupation and Materials for Role-Try-On

Vocational Role-Try-On	Image-Makers	Tools of Trade	Resources for pictures and material for boxes
CARPENTER	Work hat with cartride band for small nails and/or Carpenter's apron	folding ruler small pieces of wood, screwdriver and screws, hammer, plane, coping saw, string plans drawn from an arts and crafts book of simple things to make from wood	e.g. stilts. p. 70 *Making Things: A Handbook of Creative Discovery* by Ann Wiseman; Little, Brown and Co.

BARBER/ HAIR STYLIST	Smock	one comb for child (marked with name)	
		scissors which won't cut	
		curlers/papers	
		picture book of hair styles for girls and women	
		picture book of hair styles for boys and men	
MECHANIC	grease stained work shirt	wrench screwdriver old car parts or simple motors kit	Any local garage can provide worn out parts
		Pictures and diagrams of cross sections and/or picture diagrams from model plane and car kits	Car agency booklets

Ask model building enthusiasts for left over instructions |

Fill in the columns on the following page with your own ideas.

Vocational Role Try On	Image Makers	Tools of Trade	Resources for pictures and material for boxes
SECRETARY			
PHYSICIAN			
HOMEMAKER			

PLUMBER

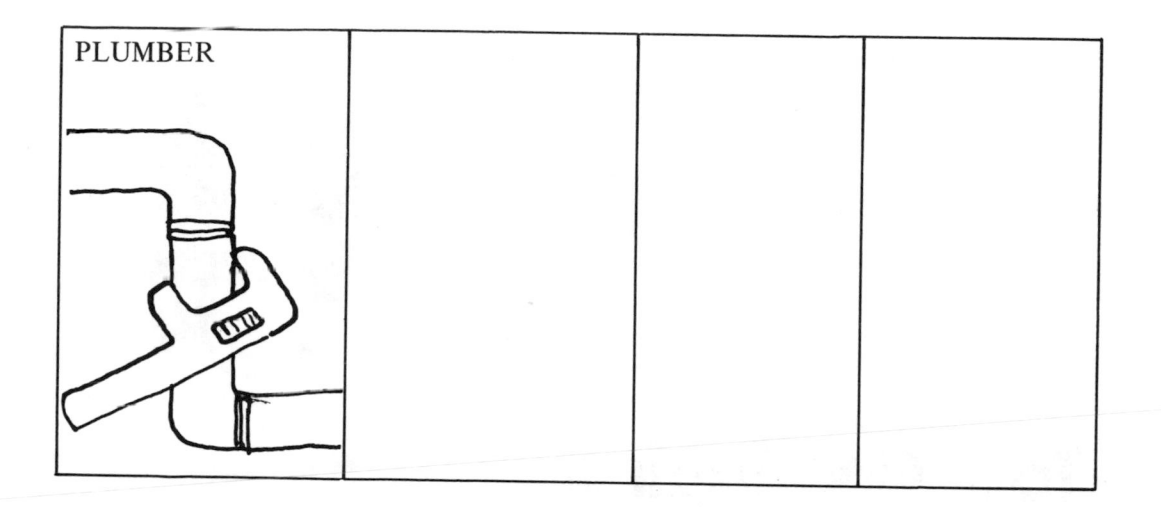

Toys And Toying

Objectives For Children:
1. To describe and compare personal feelings and reactions relative to departing from traditional sex-roles in play.
2. To identify causes and reasons for feelings.
3. To work out problem solutions for management of feelings.

Time Required:
Approximately five sessions of 30 to 45 minutes

Number Of Participants:
25-30

Materials:
1. Pictures of toys to cut out and paste (catalogs and newspaper ads).
2. Toys such as dolls, tea sets, sports equipment, cars, GI Joe, etc. (Ask children to bring their favorite toy.)
3. Newsprint and magic marker
4. One homework sheet per participant, see step 5.

Process:

1. The teacher asks children to bring a favorite toy. The results are tabulated as follows and the children are asked to look for and discuss patterns.

Girls Brought	Boys Brought	Both Girls and Boys Brought

2. The teacher asks the boys to play only with what the girls brought during free play and the girls are asked to play with what the boys brought. Children's expressed feelings are accepted, checked out and help is even given by the teacher to individual children who seek labels to describe their feelings while the teacher walks about and makes individual contact during the free play period.

3. After the free play period, the teacher, with the children, records their feelings on newsprint, as follows:

	BEFORE		AFTER	
	Boys	Girls	Boys	Girls
Happy				
Sad				
Surprised				
Disapprove				

4. The teacher distributes pictures of toys taken from catalogs, magazine advertisement sections of newspaper. Each child is asked to make two lists of toys; one most people would think are boys toys and one most people would think are girls toys.

5. For homework each child is instructed to take both lists and show one to two adults telling them it is a list of what he/she wants for Christmas (Chanukkah, birthday, etc.) then show the other list to two other adults telling them it is what they would like. Have children then circle the face on their homework sheet that they felt was most like the face of each adult as they saw the list.

	SURPRISED	DISAPPROVING	HAPPY	SAD
1. ADULT ONE				
2. ADULT TWO				
3. ADULT THREE				
4. ADULT FOUR				

6. When the children have completed the homework, they will discuss and write up their experiences as a whole. Questions to guide the discussion should help children to understand that what adults feel about what toys are for boys and girls has an influence on what toys they buy for children and what toys they encourage or discourage them from playing with.

7. Children should discuss what they might do if an adult showed disapproval about their playing with some toy that the adult thinks is an opposite sex toy. Let the children role play some of these situations, or similar ones the children originate.

You are a girl who is playing football when your grandmother calls to you. You go over to her and she tells you that ladies do not play such rough sports.

You are a boy making up a play with dolls, your father tells you that only sissies play with dolls.

The Middle Years: An Introduction

The fourteen activities in this section are presented for students from grades four through junior high. No real age levels apply because, as educators know it is no longer practical to think of boys and girls in terms of a certain age level. Instead, it becomes necessary to think of them in terms of maturity level—and maturity is an individual matter. In every class, from the fourth grade through junior high, there may be some children who are on the threshold of puberty or beyond it and some who are still young boys and girls, physically and in their thoughts and interests.

The activities in this section were written for classroom and/or counseling groups which include this wide diversity in maturity level. It still requires great skill and understanding, however, on the part of the teacher or counselor to select and adapt the proper exercise in order to meet the needs and hold the interest of his/her particular group. Therefore, along with providing background and purpose for the activities, the remarks which follow attempt to highlight the predominant needs of students in this age group.

The need for self-esteem retains its uppermost position in the student's development. But, much more self-observation of many more self-components occurs during puberty, along with vastly increased knowledge of the environment. Sets of self and world related observations are scanned together as the pre and early adolescent develops and uses abstract thinking in an effort to bring order and consistency to a world and self which is now much more complex.

REAL MEN ARE NOT EMOTIONAL AND THEY
DON'T SHOW FEAR

I HAVE EMOTIONS AND I GET SCARED

HOW CAN I BE A MAN IF I SHOW EMOTIONS
OR GET SCARED?

MEN ARE PILOTS

I WANT TO BE A PILOT

IF I'M A GIRL HOW CAN I BE A PILOT?

In this process of applying logic to understanding one's place in the world, a great deal of motivation to explore the world anew and re-evaluate self occurs. It is not coincidental, therefore, that within this same grade range, some girls first express the wish that they had been born a boy instead of a girl, and that almost all girls verbalize that boys are more capable, and stronger than they are.

It is important for girls and boys to see that each sex has value and examine carefully the stereotypic reasons they have acquired for valuing each sex, while replacing old reasons with new ones which are more likely to maintain self-esteem. Exercise twelve, "The Year 2001," seeks to accomplish this purpose within the context of one future function of sex differences—child bearing.

Exercise thirteen, "Deservedness," encourages students to examine the concept of reward allocation on the basis of sex, the equal pay for equal work question. In addition, students are also made aware that sex has had a major influence in determining their preference for other roles and activities. This, in turn, has led them to often have greater feelings of identity with groups of their own sex. This exercise gives recognition to the same sex clique formation so characteristic of this period of development. The educator is also encouraged to give this the acceptance it deserves while increasing each student's awareness that membership in the same sex cliques does not require absolute allegiance. In this same exercise students develop criteria for and are encouraged to question when exclusive membership is appropriate. They also discuss what the positive and negative effects of belonging to the same sex group are as well as understanding the effects of the excluded.

Exercise sixteen, "Tomboys and Sissies," further extends this purpose by presenting case examples of students who depart from traditional conceptions of sexrole and in so doing face ridicule. Students are asked to resolve the conflicts in the situations when they exhibit characteristic gestures of the opposite sex-role.

"Tomboys and Sissies, Level II" is intended for mature students only. It is offered to those who believe that students need to be aware of one important basis on which others judge sex-role preference and whose students can use this awareness in growth-producing ways for themselves and others.

For boys and girls alike, years surrounding puberty present critical points for acquiring particular learnings and attitudes about self. Friends begin to notice differences in each other. Girls who have been playing together for years notice that some of their friends are shooting up taller than others and that dolls and favorite games are not nearly as interesting as the opposite sex.

Gaps develop in communication and each thinks something is wrong with the others or with themselves. Some early maturers lose interest in school work; become restless over stories in readers; and bored with school projects. Instead of cooperating they may become obstreperous: test adult authority, and express resentment of what they consider too much restriction on their growing sense of independence.

Exercises fourteen and fifteen focus directly on developing student awareness of these changes taking place and the multitude of individual differences they cause in personality and behavior. Tendencies to sex-stereotype are examined in the process of enabling students to better understand and accept themselves, their peers, and the conflicts that occur in peer/adult relationships. The activities were designed to build self acceptance and decrease feelings of bewilderment, feelings of inferiority, and fears of being different.

Students who have matured and are beginning to experience the problems of early adolescence cannot be treated the same as others of their age who are still children. Working out solutions to the situations presented in exercises fourteen and fifteen should help young people recognize this and enable them to understand the reasons why "May's mother" or "John's teacher" treats them differently.

Students in this range of development also need to realize that not all boys and girls mature at the same time and that girls are usually in advance of boys. For this reason two case examples, of a late and early maturing student, are included.

Students at this stage of development need broad experiences which help them tailor their dreams to fit a realistic emerging self of which they can feel proud. This is the purpose of the "Developmental Inventory of Vocational Interest and Sex Role Appropriateness," exercise eighteen. This exercise, along with follow-up exercises, nineteen through twenty-four, has been carefully developed and tested because little is known about vocational aspirations in this age group.

Research in vocational theory tells us that students in this age period are not realistic in their choices of vocation. This is not unusual considering the diversified population. The research also tells us that discarding potential roles is more a process than a choice and that the roles discarded are those deemed inappropriate vocations is attributed to perceived sex-role appropriateness. The clearest evidence of this is presented by the unwillingness of girls to explore courses in secondary school which lead in career directions traditionally considered "masculine." While the outer bars to discrimination are being removed, educators are finding that "inner bars" called attitudes lock many girls tightly inside. Whether a girl decides to marry a doctor or become one has a great deal to do with what she considers feminine. And the bars are even closer together when looking at "blue-collar" occupations.

The Developmental Inventory of Vocational Interests and Sex Role Appropriateness Activity indicates that each individual group may differ in their vocational choices. Each instructor will have to determine how their students perceive themselves vocationally, and go on to consider broad alternatives of vocational choice with them—alternatives free from sex bias."

The "101 Quick Ways to Promote Feeling, Expression and Acceptability While Eliminating Boy-Girl Lines" presents a fantastic opportunity for the teacher to teach and deal with affect in a busy schedule so often dedicated to the "basics." In some schools students are called to form separate lines as often as five or six times a day, providing approximately a thousand different occasions for discrimination-learning tasks over a one year period. Just as a teacher wouldn't ask different ethnic groups to form separate lines, they should also be aware of classifying children on the basis of sex. By age three, students have learned to tell a boy from a girl but there are many people who by age thirty cannot tell you *what* it is they are feeling beyond good, bad, happy or sad. So take that minute before calling students to line up to present new and positive criteria for knowing people as different.

The Year 2001

Objectives For Students:
1. To identify student's stereotypes related to sex-roles.
2. To contrast their own ideas with those of others.
3. To analyze foundations of stereotypes and anticipate consequences.
4. To make interesting futuristic associations through creative writing or storytelling.

Time Required:
45 minutes

Number Of Participants:
35 maximum

Materials:
1. Dittoed student behavior descriptions, one for each student. (See at the end of Process)
2. Newsprint
3. Pencils
4. Magic markers
5. Paper

Process:

1. Inform your students that today they will act as futurists. Define the concept if necessary, naming, or allowing them to name, some famous futurists of past and present—Leonard da Vinci, Isaac Asimov, etc.

2. Distribute one ditto sheet to each student. Ask students to indicate their sex by circling in the top right corner instead of writing their name. Read the situation aloud as they read it silently. Tell them they will now have three minutes to make their decision and write the reason(s) for their choice.

3. Data may be analyzed and recorded on newsprint with the class as a whole or by a small group of students in a manner similar to that illustrated below:

Boys who chose boy	_____	_____ %
Boys who chose girl	_____	_____ %
Girls who chose boy	_____	_____ %
Girls who chose girl	_____	_____ %

Reasons for Boy Choice

1. More scientists will be needed and boys make . . .
2.

Reasons for Girl Choice

1. Women are needed for child bearing . . .
2.

4. The teacher will lead a discussion regarding the validity of the reasons given; e.g., Is it true that males make the best scientists? Why? Why not?

    Students should be encouraged to explain their reasons more fully and try to justify them. In essence then, the students will be discussing some of the common male and female stereotypes.

5. Continue the discussion by asking students to examine the numerical choice data. (The most usual pattern found is for a large number of girls to make opposite sex choices while few boys do.)* Ask students to identify and interpret the meaning of patterns in relationship to the value we ascribe to being male or female in our culture.

6. Continue the discussion by asking students if they believe that it will ever be possible for couples to select the sex child of their choice. If no student responds that such a procedure is currently possible through the use of amniocentesis, this can be mentioned and the value and implications discussed at a level appropriate to the maturity of the group. End discussion while interest still runs high and make the subsequent assignment.

7. Students should be encouraged to use their imaginations to project a future as they see it related to this topic by composing their own science fiction tales. Some titles may be written on the blackboard to get them started, such as: A WORLD OF WOMEN; A WORLD OF MEN; THE INVENTION OF THE THIRD SEX; A COUPLE WHO DEFIED THE WORLD ASSOCIATION LAW, YOUNG SCIENTIST DISCOVERS SOLUTION TO WORLD'S OVERCROWDING; etc. Students should be encouraged to share their stories.

DITTO SHEET

Circle: male   female

It was the year 2001 and the planet Earth was so crowded that the World Government Federation had made an enforceable law that every couple could have *one* child only. Scientists had perfected the process whereby it was possible for each couple to have the exact sex child they wanted—boy or girl.

Pretend that you are living at this time and that you must decide what

---

*See exercise 5 in Early Years for a description of common student responses found through testing.

your choice would be. Show your decision below and write the reason for it. Remember, you must make one choice or the other and that this is the only choice you will ever have.

My choice is:

My reason(s) is/are:

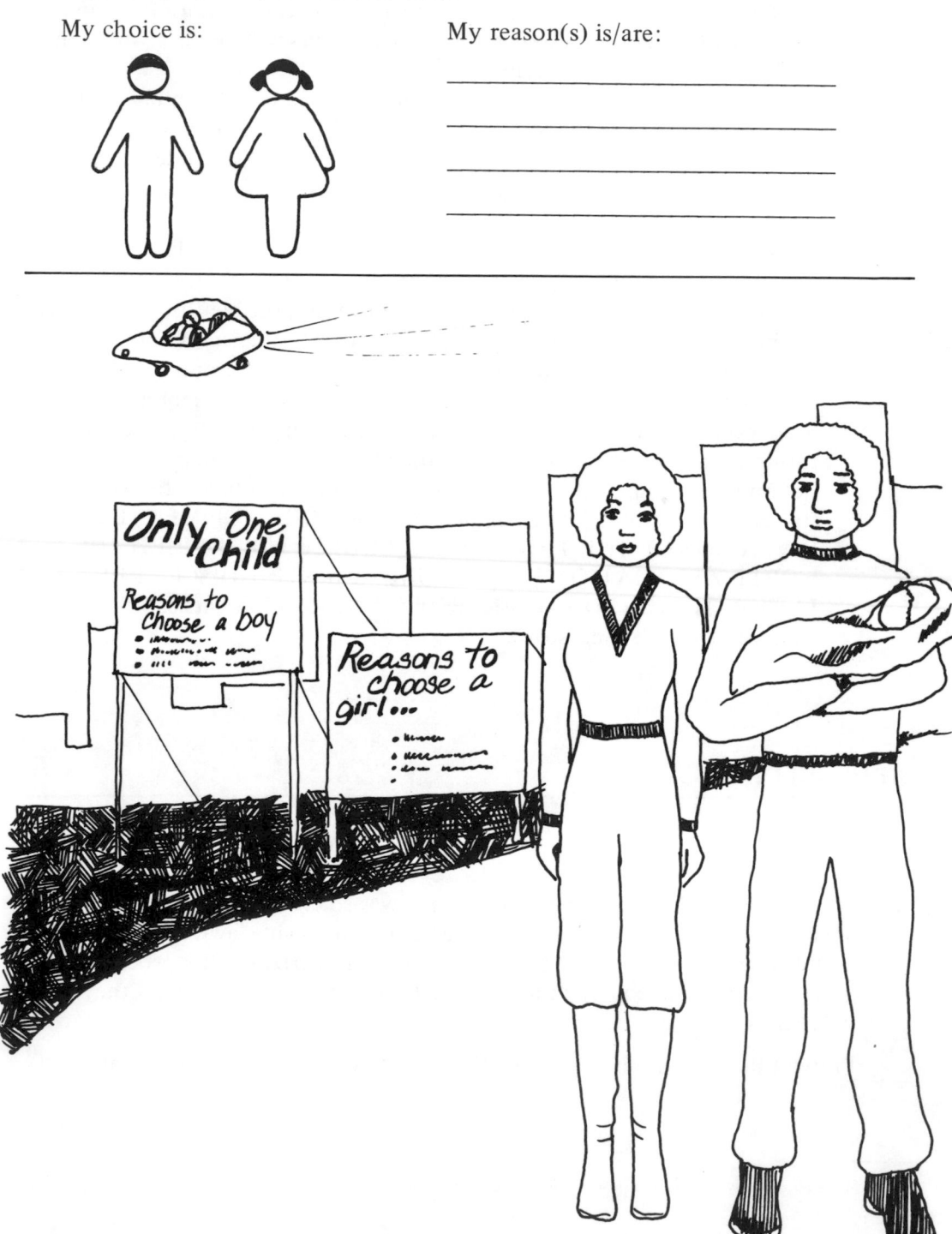

Deservedness: Who Decides And Who Gets What?

Objectives For Students:

1. To understand the concepts of intrinsic reward and extrinsic reward.
2. To identify the primary components of their own reward structure.
3. To compare and describe differences and similarities between the reward structures of boys and girls in their peer group.

Objectives For Teachers:

1. To gain a better understanding of the student peer culture and its relationship to adult world.

Time Required:

One 2-hour block with two adults, or 3 separate class periods with 1 adult.

Number Of Participants:

50 maximum

Materials:

1. One ditto sheet for each student of "The Science Fair."
2. One ditto sheet for each student of "Complete the Sentences."
3. One 3 x 5 card for each student.
4. Pencils, newsprint, magic markers

Process:
1. The teacher will introduce the activity by telling the whole class that to-day they will focus on the kinds of rewards students work for. Copies of the stimulus situation (below) will be distributed to each student with instructions to check only the response choice(s) they consider acceptable. They may check only one or more than one if their choices do not contradict each other. The results are tallied on newsprint.

DITTO SHEET

A boy and girl who lived near each other and had grown up friends decided to cooperate on a very difficult project for the Science Fair. They both worked especially hard at planning and building the project. They worked many long, hard hours after school for a month before the project was finished. Their hard work paid off and they won first prize in the state. They both had their pictures in the paper and were interviewed on TV. There was only one problem: first prize included a plane ticket to attend the World Science Fair with a teacher chaperone, and there was only one student ticket and not enough time to raise money for another.

Who should get the ticket?

[ ] The boy should go because he probably worked harder.

[ ] The girl should go because it takes more effort for a girl to succeed in science.

[ ] The girl should go because girls need more reinforcement to remain in the science field.

[ ] The girl should go because there will be many more opportunities available to the boy.

[ ] The boy should let the girl go as a matter of courtesy and good manners.

[ ] The girl should let the boy go out of respect for the science field being primarily male.

[ ] A member of the girl's family should buy a ticket and let the boy use the teacher's ticket.

[ ] None of the above answers are acceptable.

2. A teacher led discussion follows with teacher remarks confined to stimulating and guiding the discussion along two main themes: which response choices treat boys and girls unequally? (All but the last.) Is such treatment justifiable? Students should be allowed to express and defend their positions.

3. The stimulus situation can be used to teach the concepts of intrinsic and extrinsic reward. Students can be asked to identify the extrinsic rewards (recognition through TV and newspaper, ticket, winning) and intrinsic reward (the work itself when accompanied by positive feelings).

   Further ask students to consider what would happen to one sex's motivation if the other sex got the reward.

4. Ask boys and girls to list on a 3 x 5 card distributed what activities they would do which are rewarding in and of themselves.

5. Give each person a chance to read at least one of their choices and list these in summary form on newsprint sheets separately for boys and girls. Have students study the sheets and circle those which boys and girls have in common. Then discuss possible reasons for differences.

   The teacher will expect and accept differences as a matter of student preference pointing out that this is one main reason why boys prefer to be with boys and girls with girls. We all prefer to be with people who share our interests. Ask students to consider if there are any dangers in this? Students will usually come up with two and be ready to discuss solutions: (1) a group isolated from the larger group constricts thinking and acceptance; (2) interest groups are artificial if interests cross sex lines and members of one sex are excluded or considered odd if they try to be included.

   The teacher should try to lead discussion away from premature discussions of what *ought to be* in order to facilitate student awareness in the following parts of this exercise that these preferences are largely the result of early conditioning; that is, boys and girls learn what is "suitable" for them to be interested in from those around them and the media.

6. Students will be divided into separate sex groups. Students will jot notes for themselves by each item on the "Complete the Sentences" blank which should now be distributed.

DITTO SHEET

COMPLETE THE SENTENCES

1. I can usually get my father's approval or make him smile if I

_____

2. I can usually get my mother's approval or make her smile if I

   _____

3. My father gets mad or punishes me if I _____

   _____

4. My mother gets mad or punishes me if I _____

   _____

5. Boys don't like girls who _____

6. Boys don't like boys who _____

7. Girls don't like boys who _____

8. Girls don't like girls who _____

---

7. While still in separate sex groups, students will share their thoughts c
   above with the teacher who makes a summary listing on newsprint.
8. The boys and girls will now meet together as a total group comparing
   newsprint summary sheets. Boys or girls may ask for or be given mo
   complete explanations of any of the things listed. The exercise is co
   pleted by inviting participants to share reactions to the activity.

Self-Enhancing Prophecies: Level I

Objectives For Students:

1. To identify the following common concerns and conflictual situations which confront pre- and early adolescents as important to many persons' self-definitions, regardless of sex: early maturer, later maturer, crushes, individual vs. group, relations to authority, embarrassment before peers.
2. To begin to discriminate how use of the following behaviors can increase maturity or retard it: conformity-cooperation; imagination-daydreaming; dominance and leadership; empathy and autonomy.
3. To recognize expectancies for particular behavior and personality traits to be more characteristic of one sex and the potential consequences of such expectancies.
4. To problem solve common conflictual situations for growth-producing solutions; e.g., when is conformity positive, when negative?
5. To increase empathy and tolerance for wide diversity of persons and behaviors in peer age groups.

Objectives For Teachers:

1. To identify problem areas of particular concern for curriculum or student development planning.
2. To identify structure of student's values and preferences for particular personality and behavior traits.
3. To identify indications of what students consider best treatment of common problems.

Time Required:
Four class periods of 50 minutes

Number Of Participants:
40 maximum

Materials:
1. Dittoed student behavior descriptions, one for each student.
2. Answer blank to accompany the above.
3. Newsprint sheets, magic markers and pencils.

Process:
For teacher's information: G, B, and P portray personality and behavioral qualities which are essentially positive but presented in a conflictual situation, while O and D present potential problems due to physical maturity. Titles are, then: G-Positive conformity/cooperation; B-Creative leadership; P-Assertive; O-Late maturer; and D-Early maturer.

1. The teacher introduces the activity by explaining that students will be reading behavior descriptions of five students in their age range but that the sex of the student has been concealed. Students are asked to read each and after reading, check under the appropriate column in the answer blank.

2. Student Descriptions and Student Description Answer Blanks are distributed and students are asked to indicate what sex they are at the top of the answer blank.

3. Volunteers are chosen to collect and summarize the data from the answer blanks onto newsprint sheets. The headed newsprint sheets should be shown so that students will understand what information will be presented for discussion at a later time.

Headed Sample Newsprint Sheets

Sex Guesses	
B	
boy	girl
7	29
O	
boy	girl

No. of Choices			
A	B	C	D
B 9	11	16	-
O 2	7	7	-

Headed Sample Newsprint Sheets

When a Boy Guessed Boy*	When a Boy Guessed Boy*
Want for a Friend	Like myself
B Yes 32 No 4	B Yes 7 No ___ Somewhat 27
O Yes ___ No ___	O Yes ___ No ___ Somewhat ___

3. Enough time should be allowed for discussion of each student description. The teacher should guide the discussion so that the following points emerge: All cases deal with trusting yourself (i.e., am I okay?). What are the effects of not doing this? What were the positive behaviors of each description? What were the group influences in each description? What is a counselor's (psychologist, etc.) job? When should a student see one? What does it mean to get professional help?

4. When volunteers have completed tabulating student answers on newsprint they will present the summarized data. Each newsprint sheet should be discussed through teacher questioning and student problem solving. (For example: sex guesses.) Whenever the number of sex guesses were not equal for a particular student description, question as to why. Have students explain their reasons. Ask students to give illustrations of what expectancies are, and what effects they can cause. Then, ask how do you think expecting boys to be more dominant, for example, affects some boys? Affects girls?

---

*Three other newsprint sheets are needed. Their headings will differ in that the first line will read:
    (1) When a boy guessed a girl
    (2) When a girl guessed a girl
    (3) When a girl guessed a boy

STUDENT DESCRIPTIONS

Number 1 — G

G's friend has just said G is always too good and that others will take advantage of G. "You've got to be more aggressive. No one else would have turned that $5 in to the office like you did. That was dumb. The person that lost it doesn't expect to get it back. Somebody in that office will probably just end up getting the money when you could have used it. Anyone else would have kept it."

Now G thinks of the friend's advice, for G has just agreed to share an important science resource book that G checked out and needs in order to make the Science Fair project that G expects and wants badly to win first place. The student who asked G to let him use it half time is G's most likely competitor for first place.

After G agrees, G thinks: "Maybe my friend is right; maybe I'm not aggressive enough. Should I try to change?"

Do you think G is a male or a female?

What should G do?

a. Trust self-judgement. G is fine as is.
b. Accept friend's advice from now on and try to become more aggressive.

Number 2 — P

P and five other friends were organizing their own club.

1st friend: Hey, why don't we ask Pat to join?

P: No way.

2nd friend: But, Pat can be a lot of fun sometimes.

P: Yeah, and a lot of weird the rest. Pat's out, that's final. What kind of club have we got if we let every dummy in.

3rd friend: We're going to get accused of being an exclusive club and that's against school rules.

P: No, we're not. For one thing, we're not meeting at school, and for another, all of you can just keep quiet about it. It's nobody's business but ours.

4th friend: Supposing they find out?

P: They won't, but even if they do, they can't do anything. The Constitution guarantees everyone the right to choose their own friends. Okay, now I'll be the president and you can . . .

    2nd friend: Wait a minute! How come you're president?

    P: Because it was my idea to begin with and we're meeting at my house.

    2nd friend: We can meet at my house, too.

    4th friend: Yeah, why don't we take turns meeting at each other's houses.

    P: Great. Now that that's all settled, let's get going and plan our first party. Okay?

    All others: Yah, great, when are we going to have it?

    P: I thought right after the next basketball game would be good. Any objections?

None of the others object, and the planning continues.

Do you think P is a male or a female?

Which choice identifies P's positive behaviors?

a. Accepts ideas of others.
b. Has ideas and is knowledgeable; takes initiative; organizes activities of others.
c. Both a and b above.
d. None of above. P shows no positive behaviors in the above situation.

Number 3 — B

    B is always brimming with ideas. As a matter of fact, most of the other kids like B, because of B's gobs of plans to do things. Sometimes without realizing what's happening, they go along with the activities B starts. B has tons of energy. B gets what B wants by gently bossing others or planning in such a way that they carry out B's projects.

    B talked the teacher into letting a group of the kids use some free time in school to practice a play B had written for creative writing. The teacher had read the play so she said it was okay to present it to the rest of the class and invite other classes.

    The students brought their costumes and scenery they had made. But when the play was presented, the teacher realized that B had deliberately chosen two of the ugliest girls to play witches and a fat boy to play a part which made everyone laugh at his fatness.

Do you think B is a male or a female?

What should be done to B?

a. Teacher should choose a play which has a role for an evil schemer or devil and let another group practice and put it on, but make sure B plays the evil part.
b. B should be praised for his/her accomplishment but taken aside to discuss it would feel to be in the shoes of the others in the play.
c. Nothing.
d. B should be punished by separating him/her from activities with a group for a long while.

Number 4 – O

The other kids began to notice that O had a crush on the teacher. O did a lot of soulful gazing; asking to run unnecessary errands and brushing against the teacher whenever possible. O pretended not to care what they thought; but O cared: O cared particularly since the other kids were more mature and group dating. About the only place O felt like a star was in daydreams.

One day O dropped a picture in the cafeteria and before it could be picked up, one kid grabbed it and called to all the rest: "O's got a picture of the teacher!" The other kids started chanting: "O's in love with teacher! O's in love with teacher!" O felt hot all over and turned to walk away fast, but saw the teacher had heard and seen everything.

Do you think O is male or female?

What should be done?

a. O should seek help from counselor or someone who works especially with kids who have problems.
b. O should ignore the kids' teasing. It won't last, and neither will O's problem. O is just late maturing.
c. O should see a doctor for a physical check-up and meanwhile try to get involved with what kids his age are doing, even if O has to fake interest.
d. O should ignore the other kids and learn to handle things alone.

STUDENT DESCRIPTION ANSWER BLANKS

Student	Student's Sex	Best Response A	B	C	D	I would have as a friend Yes	No	Like myself Yes	No	Somewhat
G	M F	( )	( )	( )	( )	( )	( )	( )	( )	( )
P	M F	( )	( )	( )	( )	( )	( )	( )	( )	( )
B	M F	( )	( )	( )	( )	( )	( )	( )	( )	( )
O	M F	( )	( )	( )	( )	( )	( )	( )	( )	( )
D	M F	( )	( )	( )	( )	( )	( )	( )	( )	( )

What You See Is What You Get: Level II

Objectives For Students:
1. To identify any expectancies for the following negative behaviors to be sex biased: submissiveness, dependency, withdrawal, undependable, unattractive, aggressive.
2. To acquire information regarding the above negative behaviors.
3. To develop skills in problem solving for more positive emotional growth.
4. To develop attitudes of viewing persons who display negative behaviors from a need to understand rather than condemn.

Objectives For Teachers:
1. To identify problem areas of particular concern for curriculum or student development planning.
2. To identify structure of student's values and preferences for particular personality and behavior traits.
3. To identify indications of what students consider best treatment of common problems.

Time Required:
Minimum of 3 class periods

Number Of Participants:
40 minimum

Materials:
1. Student behavior descriptions, one for each student.
2. Student behavior description answer blank.
3. Newsprint, magic markers and pencils.

Process:

For the teacher's information: Select one or all of the student descriptions appropriate for your groups needs. R = aggressive; H = submissive; Q = dependent; A = withdrawing; C = unattractive; and J = undependable.

1. The teacher distributes the dittoed behavior descriptions and answer blanks, telling students that they will be reading short descriptions of six students and deciding what would be helpful for each student's future growth. The teacher adds that the responses they have to choose from are too simple but that they should select the one that in their opinion is the best of the four. Students are also informed that they will have a chance to add their own ideas later. Students should understand they do not have to sign their names on the answer blank—only sex designation.
2. After students have had a chance to respond to each behavior description, volunteers are chosen to collect and summarize the data from the answer blanks onto newsprint sheets. The headed newsprint sheets are shown so that the class members will understand what information will be presented for discussion at a later time.

SAMPLE OF NEWSPRINT DATA ANALYSIS SHEETS

SEX GUESSES				NUMBER OF CHOICES			
				A	B	C	D
R	M 41	F 9		R 12	24	13	1
H	M 7	F 43		H ___	___	___	___
Q	____	____		Q ___	___	___	___

SAMPLE OF NEWSPRINT DATA ANALYSIS SHEETS

When a Boy Guessed Boy:* Want for a Friend			When a Boy Guessed Boy:* Like myself		
R	Yes 17	No 9	R	Yes 21	No 5
H	Yes ___	No ___	H	Yes ___	No ___
Q	Yes ___	No ___	Q	Yes ___	No ___

3. While student response data is being summarized, the total group is divided into small groups of three to five. Each group is assigned a different student description with the particular sex designation now specified. For each student description assigned to one group as male, ensure that another group has that same student description and has been told to assume it is a female.

Instructions to each small group:

a. read the description once again
b. decide how this person could best help themselves
c. decide what others could do to help
d. be ready to present these solutions to the whole group

4. The teacher will call on the small groups to report out their suggestions. The groups should report in pairs and subsequent to each pair, class members should comment on whether the groups' suggestions differed because of sex and if so, why, and what effect would each suggestion have on a member of that sex.

5. Presentation of summarized data: when the volunteers have the data from the student answer blanks cumulated on newsprint, they should present it to the class. The class should discuss any patterns and the implications of same for each set of newsprint data.

---

*Three other newsprint sheets are needed. Their headings will differ in that the first line will read:

When a boy guessed girl
When a girl guessed boy
When a girl guessed girl

BEHAVIOR DESCRIPTIONS

Number 1 — R

R is sent to the principal's office for disciplinary action by R's teacher. R explains to the principal, "All the time she asks me to do my work over because she says it's too messy . . . I don't think being neat is so important. Then today I just got mad at some kids who were laughing at my report. The teacher said ignore them, but who can do that? I didn't get fresh . . . well, not at first anyway. I didn't call her stupid until she started pushing me into my seat."

Do you think R is male or female?

What should be done?

  a. The principal should apply the paddle but explain why first.

  b. The principal should advise R to find better ways to handle frustration and suggest the student apologize. Before the student returns suggest to the teacher alone other ways to handle it.

  c. Inform R that it was wrong to fight and call names and give R a cooling off period before returning to class.

  d. Change R to another class.

Number 2 — H

Friend: Where's your guitar?

H: I gave it to Pat to use.

Friend: Why did you do that, now you don't have one to use when we get to class.

H. Pat asked for it. I didn't want to say no. Besides, I can listen and watch. Maybe I could use yours part of the time.

Friend: No way; I'm no dummy like you are. You even give in when kids ask for your lunch money. You just hand it right over like they were really your friends.

H: I don't always.

Friend: Name one time you refused . . . See, you can't. Hey, since you don't have anything to carry, how about carrying my case.

H: [taking friend's case afterall] Promise, promise I can use it; otherwise you'll say you didn't.

Friend: I said maybe. I'll see how I feel when we get there. If the teacher has an extra, then you can . . .

H: Okay.

Is H a male or a female?

What should be done?

a. H should try to make new friends.
b. H should not worry so much about being liked and begin standing up for self.
c. Nothing. H is pretty okay.

Number 3 — Q

Q sat crying at a desk as the late afternoon sun streamed into the empty classroom.

Teacher: [Enters and looks at Q sympathetically] What's wrong now?

Q: Nothing . . . Oh, everything. I'm so miserably lonely!

Teacher: But you have so many friends.

Q: You mean the kids I run around with? They're so phony (face grows angry). You don't know how they play games. I'm sure they seem okay to you the way they act interested in everything you say and laugh at your jokes, but you should hear them outside. (Breaks down in tears again.) There's just no one who really likes me.

Teacher: What about Pat? You two seem pretty close.

Q: Pat acts like a friend but can't wait to put me down . . . always does. Just today I asked Pat how my project looked before finishing and just like that, criticism: "the seams aren't joined well." Some friend! I haven't anyone I can trust. [More crying.]

Teacher: [Warmly] I think you know you can trust me.

Q: [Brightens] Can I really! (Then sobering.) Do you really like me or are you just saying that to make me feel good? You can tell me. I really want to know.

Do you think Q is male or female?

What should be done?

a. Q should try to make a new group of friends.

b. Q should not think so much about friends and try to become more independent.

c. Nothing. It's probably just a mood. Q will feel differently tomorrow.

Number 4 — A

A is thin and taller than most others in the class, and yet you can easily forget A when trying to think of whom to invite to a party or in choosing up sides for a game. A is never rude or impatient with others like some in the class, and yet A has only one friend. This friend lives near A and they talk and run around together a lot. But if some other kids call A's friend to join them, the friend goes and forgets all about A. One time A visited Mexico and brought back a ring to show the class. When A got to school A could not get the courage to tell the teacher, but A's friend did and then the teacher had A tell everyone about the trip and show the ring. All the kids wanted a chance to use it. Almost everyone had a chance. However, when it was time to go home, the ring had disappeared. A said nothing, but for the next three mornings A played sick. After that A would leave for school, but never arrive. Instead A wandered around in the woods nearby. When A's family found out, A flatly refused to ever return to school. A cried and swore A hated everyone there and they hated A too. Short of carrying A bodily to the class, there was no way A's family could make A go to school.

Do you think A is a male or female?

What should be done?

a. Let A change schools to one with more friendly students who will not treat A this way.

b. Make A return to school . . . *but* changes will have to be made in the teacher and A's behavior.

c. A's family must become closer and try to make A feel really loved.

Number 5 — C

If you were to come up to a group of kids you'd never met before, C is the one person in the group you would probably not try to get to know. C just doesn't appeal to people at first. C is usually the one who stands stooped over or leaning against the wall. C rarely laughs or smiles and when speaking has a thin, almost whiny voice. If you did try to catch C's eye to talk, you would not be able to be-cause C avoids looking at most people. C has large ears, bumpy skin and a nose too long for the face.

C didn't want to go to the first boy-girl party one of the kids gave, but did because it was a friend and the friend's birthday. The kids at the party danced for two hours. Two miserable agonizing hours for C who slouched on the side the whole time because no one would dance with C. Then C went home and cried.

Do you think C is a male or female?

What should be done?

a. C should have a physical check-up, and begin practicing good health and grooming habits.
b. C should concentrate energies on becoming an excellent student. C will win recognition through achievement, not popularity.
c. C's family should take C in hand, telling C how to dress and make the most of C's positive features.

Number 6 – J

J wasn't stupid at all, even though J was getting poor grades. The difficulty with J was getting things started; then once they were started, getting them finished. J always had good intentions, in fact, was known for having a kind heart. That's probably why J had friends. Currently, two of J's friends are waiting out-side the school. J had to stay after to talk with Miss Scott about history. J comes out the door obviously upset and fighting tears.

Friends: What happened?

J: [hardly able to answer] She's going to fail me. My family's going to kill me! I'm failing. Here's the notice I have to take home and get signed. (Tears finally, and panic.)

1st friend: This just says you're going to fail if you don't get all your missing homework in.

J: [Wailing] But I can't do it; there's too much. I'm going to split. My folks will kill me. I told them I didn't have any homework.

2nd friend: Look, you can have my old papers again. Just make a few mis-takes this time so she won't be suspicious.

J: Hey, thanks, you saved my life. (Panic strikes J's eyes again.) Ohhh—

1st friend: Now what?

102

J: The test! I can't pass the final test! (J looks about to cry when an idea strikes.) Would you help? We could all study together. You two could be teachers. You know what questions to ask and if we did cram together I know I . . .

The two friends object, stating that J talks too much about other things and fools around when they study, but after J pleads over and over, promising to work, they give in.

Is J a male or female?

Which of the following would be best for J?

a. J's friends should continue to help him as they agreed so that J can learn from their good example.

b. J's family and teachers should put the pressure on him earlier so J develops better study habits right along.

c. J should be allowed to experience the consequences of his poor study habits.

BEHAVIOR DESCRIPTION ANSWER BLANK

Student	Student's Sex	A	B	C	D	I would have as a friend Yes	No	Like myself A lot	A little	Not
R	M F	( )	( )	( )	( )	( )	( )	( )	( )	( )
H	M F	( )	( )	( )	( )	( )	( )	( )	( )	( )
Q	M F	( )	( )	( )	( )	( )	( )	( )	( )	( )
A	M F	( )	( )	( )	( )	( )	( )	( )	( )	( )
C	M F	( )	( )	( )	( )	( )	( )	( )	( )	( )
J	M F	( )	( )	( )	( )	( )	( )	( )	( )	( )

Tomboys And Sissies 1

Objectives For Students:
1. To be sensitized to factors involved when trying out new or less traditional sex-roles.
2. To increase skill in problem solving.
3. To increase self-expression by non-abstract means.

Time Required:
150 minutes, or 2 to 3 class periods

Number Of Participants:
60 maximum

Materials:
1. Each anecdotal situation put on separate cards.

Process:
1. Anecdotal situations for problem solving are presented below in five pairs.

In each pairing the situations remain nearly identical while the sex of the student varies. The teacher should select those paired anecdotal situations which seem most appropriate to the needs and the maturity level of his/her students.

2. Members of the total group should be divided into small mixed sex groups of four to six students. There will need to be an even number of groups because the situations to solve are paired (without student awareness). Each group should be instructed to choose a discussion leader and the leader's role explained.

3. The leader in each group will be asked to read the problem situation. The group members will then try to reach consensus about a resolution through discussion. Allow from 15-20 minutes.*

4. The leader from each group will then present the problem with its resolution to the total group.

5. The class will react to each problem solution; most particularly noting contrasts that occur when only the sex differs in the same situation, but also commenting on the quality of the resolution.

6. Students should be asked to take note of the sex of the discussion leaders and discuss possible meanings if a patterning by sex has occurred.

ANECDOTAL SITUATIONS

1A Jorge is almost always afraid of something. Sometimes he is afraid of things which it seems likely could never happen. Other times when he seems worried or upset, he can't give any reason for it. His teacher is concerned enough to request a parent conference. The parents tell her that he is not this way at home, but that often in the morning he does not want to go to school; complaining that the girls always seem to do everything better than he does.

What would be a good way to help Jorge be less fearful?

1B Alicia is almost always afraid of something. Sometimes she is afraid of things which it seems likely could never happen. Other times when she seems worried or upset, she can't give any reason for it. Her teacher is concerned enough to request a parent conference. The parents tell her that she is not this way at home, but that often in the morning she says she wants to stay home because the boys are too rough and mean at school.

What would be a good way to help Alicia be less fearful?

---

*This exercise may be altered by using the anecdotal situations for role play.

2A   Mary wants to join the boys at basketball during recess. The boys refuse to allow her to play and the kids all call her weird.

How would you solve this problem?

2B   John wants to join the girls at jumping rope during recess. The girls refuse to allow him to play and the kids all call him weird.

How would you solve this problem?

3A   Joe, a fifth grade boy, helps his mother to do all the household chores: dusting, vacuuming, washing dishes, cooking, mending and sorting the laundry. The other children in the class find out about this and they laugh and tease him.

What should be done?

3B   Michelle, a fifth grade girl, has a paper route and is the only girl in school to have one. The other children in the class find out about this and they laugh and tease her.

What should be done?

4A   A father drops off his sixth grade son at school every day and kisses the boy goodbye. The other children see and laugh.

What should be done?

4B   A girl in the sixth grade changes in the girls' bathroom in preparation for her Karate class, to which her mother takes her directly after picking her up. The other children see and laugh.

What should be done?

5A   In the first couple of months of school you observe that one of the students, Patrick, likes to show everyone how tough he is. On the playground, he always tries to take the lead in games and frequently succeeds in filling the dominant role. Surprisingly, the boys don't seem to mind Patrick's dominance. At least they haven't visibly complained yet. On a few occasions, Patrick has gotten into fights, though, with the other students, but the causes seem to be related to other things.

What should be done?

5B   In the first couple of months of school you observe that Patricia, one of the students, likes to show everyone how tough she is. On the playground she always tries to take the lead in games and frequently succeeds in filling the dominant role.

Surprisingly, the boys don't seem to mind Patricia's dominance. At least, there have been no visible complaints. On a few occasions Patricia has gotten into fights with others in the class, but the causes seem to be related to other things.

What should be done?

Tomboys And Sissies II

Objectives For Students:
1. To describe and compare personal feelings and reactions of others relative to non-verbal behaviors; most especially, non-verbal departures from traditional sex-role gestures.
2. To be sensitized to expressions of social approval and disapproval and their effects on conditioning male and female characteristics.
3. To discriminate differences in use of common non-verbal gestures by males and females.
4. To be sensitized to the generalizations applied to persons from a relatively few bits of non-verbal information.

Time Required:
Two 50 minute periods

Number Of Participants:
A carefully selected small group of students who are mature and concerned with positive development of their sex-role identity.

Materials:
1. One non-verbal data card for each student. See step 4.

Process:

1. As preparation for this exercise, the facilitator tells students that it has been found that persons who maintain eye contact and smile in their interaction with adults receive much more positive judgements from these adults about their intelligence and their "likeability."*

2. The facilitator asks students to form groups of three and distributes a topic for each group to use as a basis for conversation. Each member of the resulting triad is to take turns completing the following roles which are described by the teacher.

   a. Role Player—The task of the role-player is to carry on his/her part of the conversation with the role receiver while maintaining a neutral face and little if any eye contact.

   b. Role Receiver—The task of the role receiver is to carry on a conversation with the role-player.

   c. Observer—The task of the observer is to observe both the role-player and role receiver during their conversation. Following it the observer reports to the role player his/her effectiveness in maintaining role and reports to role receiver non-verbal reactions observed.

   Approximately three minutes should be devoted to the conversation and two minutes to the observer's feedback, then the facilitator announces: "Please switch roles." In five more minutes the facilitator will again ask students to switch roles, thus allowing each member of the triad to experience all three roles.

3. Students are asked to form new groups of three. Again, each member of the triad is to take turns completing the three roles. The difference this time is that the task of the role player is to carry on the conversation with as much eye contact as possible and with as many smiles as can be made to seem natural.

4. The total group comes together to share their reactions, after which time they are asked to try *both* roles with adults; recording the results on the non-verbal data cards distributed. (See next page.)

---

*Nancy L. Cantor and Donna M. Gelfand, "Effects of Responsiveness and Sex of Children on Adult Behavior," *Child Development*, 1977, *48*, 232-238.

```
┌─────────────────────────────────────────────────────────────────────┐
│                        NON-VERBAL DATA CARD                           │
│                                                                       │
│   Adult #1    Hold two separate conversations with a time interval    │
│               between.  At one time, use little eye contact or        │
│               smiling.  At the other time, use a lot.                 │
│   ─────────────────────────────────────────────────────────────────  │
│   Adults reaction    When I      When I                               │
│                      was:        was:        Describe the reaction:   │
│   ─────────────────────────────────────────────────────────────────  │
│   Positive                                                            │
│   ─────────────────────────────────────────────────────────────────  │
│   Negative                                                            │
│   ═════════════════════════════════════════════════════════════════  │
│   Adult #2                                                            │
│   ─────────────────────────────────────────────────────────────────  │
│   Positive                                                            │
│   ─────────────────────────────────────────────────────────────────  │
│   Negative                                                            │
│   ─────────────────────────────────────────────────────────────────  │
└─────────────────────────────────────────────────────────────────────┘
```

5. This homework assignment is followed up with a discussion which includes the following:

   a. How did the adults show positive reactions, negative reactions; verbally and non-verbally?
   b. What effects does this have on the way you consciously present myself now?
   c. Is it valid for people to make negative assumptions on the basis of such a small amount of non-verbal data?

6. A similar procedure is now carried out as regards sex typed gestures only this time the exercise is terminated without a homework assignment.

7. The teacher gives the students the following information:

   Some research results strongly indicate that there are three gestures which discriminate between the sexes, and a fourth which very likely does, too.* These are:

limp wrist (feminine)	— flexing the wrist toward the palmar surface of the forearm and/or upper arm while the elbow is either flexed or extended.

---

*George A. Rekers, Hortensia D. Amaro-Plotkin, and Benson P. Low, "Sex Typed Mannerisms in Normal Boys and Girls as a Function of Sex and Age," *Child Development*, 1977, *48*, 275-278.

arm flutters (feminine)	— a rapid succession of up-and-down movements of the forearm and/or upper arm while the wrist remains relaxed.
flexed elbow (feminine)	— walking or standing with the arm(s) held such that the angle between the forearm and the upper arm is between 90° and 135°.
hands on hips (feminine)	— Girls either place the hands on the hips with the palms turned up and the fingers pointing to the rear, or put the hands on the upper part of the hips with the palms facing down and the fingers pointing down and to the rear.
(masculine)	Boys usually place the hands on the hips with the palms facing down and the fingers pointing forward.

8. Students are asked to form groups of three to once again hold a conversation on a topic. At least one male is included in each triad. The male becomes the role player whose task it is to simulate the "feminine" gestures. The other two members will be the role receiver and observer respectively. After five minutes the teacher will ask all members of the triad to share their reactions and feedback with each other.

9. The total group comes together to share their reactions and discuss the same points included in Step 5. In addition, students are asked to consider why girls were not asked to simulate "male" gestures and what reactions they would expect from adults and peers *if* they were given a similar assignment like the one with facial expressions and eye contact.

Beginning With The Students Vocational Perceptions: The Developmental Inventory Of Vocational Interest And Sex Role Appropriateness

18

Objectives For Students:

1. To determine the relationship of student's occupational interests to their perceptions of vocational sex-role appropriateness.
2. To measure the developing occupational interests of students.

Time Required:

Two class periods of 50 minutes

Number Of Participants:

Maximum 50 students

Materials:

1. Directions for administration of the Developmental Inventory of Vocational Interest and Sex Role Appropriateness (DIVISRA), Appendix A.
2. Student Response inventories: one set for each student.
3. Pencils, magic marker, newsprint, and Class Data Analysis Form.

Process:

1. The student response blanks are distributed; making sure the last column is folded back on each blank. The DIVISRA is then administered according to the directions (Appendix A).

2. The teacher asks students to raise their hands so that he/she can count and record quickly the information called for on the Class Data Analysis Form. These columns from left to right are:

First: Number of girls who see this as a male's job only.

Second: Number of girls who see this as a female's job only.

Third: Number of girls who would like this job.

Fourth: Number of girls who would not like this job.

Fifth: Number of boys who see this as a male's job only.

Sixth: Number of boys who see this as a female's job only.

Seventh: Number of boys who would like this job.

Eighth: Number of boys who would not like this job.

Ninth: Number of girls who would like this job, but see it as best done by a male.

Tenth: Number of girls who would not like this job, but see it as female work.

Eleventh: Number of boys who would like this job but see it as best done by a female.

Twelfth: Number of boys who would not like this job, but see it as male's work.

Teacher's Name _____

School _____

CLASS DATA ANALYSIS FORM

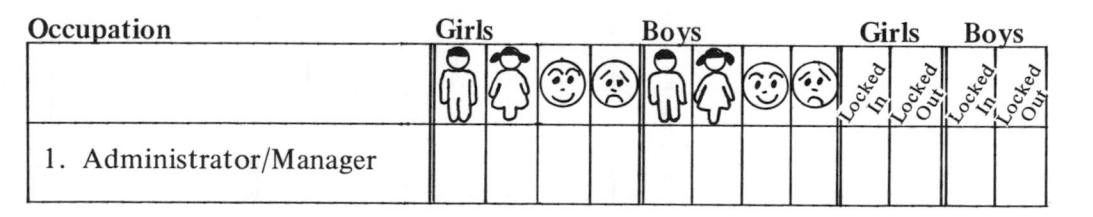

Occupation	Girls				Boys				Girls		Boys	
									Locked In	Locked Out	Locked In	Locked Out
1. Administrator/Manager												

Occupation	Girls				Boys				Girls		Boys	
									Locked In	Locked Out	Locked In	Locked Out
2. Barber/Hair Stylist												
3. Carpenter												
4. Child Care Worker												
5. Dentist												
6. Engineer												
7. Entertainer												
8. Factory Worker												
9. Farmer												
10. Firefighter												
11. Food Service Worker												
12. Garbage Collector												
13. Homemaker												
14. Housecleaner												
15. Landscaper												
16. Lawyer												
17. Mail Carrier												
18. Maintenance Worker												

Occupation	Girls				Boys				Girls		Boys	
									Locked In	Locked Out	Locked In	Locked Out
19. Mechanic												
20. Minister, Priest, Rabbi												
21. Nurse												
22. Physician												
23. Pilot												
24. Plumber												
25. Police Officer												
26. President of U.S.												
27. Real Estate Agent												
28. Repairer/Installer												
29. Road Worker												
30. Sales Clerk												
31. Sales Representative												
32. Secretary												
33. Soldier												
34. Teacher												
35. Telephone Operator												
36. Truck Driver												

Why Not?

Objectives For Students:
1. To analyze those occupations they perceived as most stereotyped for men and women as measured by the DIVISRA.
2. To share their perceptions of each other in terms of personal qualifications for occupations.
3. To refine specific questions about occupations; research these and share the information.

Time Required:
75 minutes minimum or two class periods

Number Of Participants:
Between 30 and 40

Materials:
1. Newsprint posted which identifies the 15 most stereotyped occupations of males and females (taken from Class Data Analysis Form of Exercise 18).

Process:

1. The students will be asked to choose a partner. Each partner will take turns completing the roles described below:

   a. **Giver**—The *Giver* is to share his/her perception of the Receiver in terms of one of the stereotyped occupations which is *not* the receiver's sex (i.e., "I think you might well consider becoming a lawyer [to a girl]. Or a politician."). The Giver must also give his/her reasons for stating the occupation(s). ("You are able to get many of the kids in this class to go along with your ideas and you have a mind that seems to see all the arguments ahead plus you argue well enough to make your point.")

   b. **Receiver**—The *Receiver* listens to the Giver's perception and then shares his/her reaction to it. (i.e., "I would like being a politician but I wouldn't want to be a lawyer because it takes too much schooling.")

   Approximately three minutes should be devoted to each role above. After three minutes, teacher announces, "Please switch roles—if you were the Giver, you are now the Receiver." Allow another three minutes.

2. The teacher will ask each set of partners to join with two other sets for a total of six in a group. Teacher will instruct students to go around the circle letting each person tell what jobs their partner saw as possible for them; the reasons their partner gave; and their own reactions. Other members of the circle will be asked to share their feedback (e.g., agree, disagree, questioning why someone does or doesn't, etc.).

3. After thirty minutes, or in the next class session, the teacher will call the class together and ask what questions were raised about occupations which need further answers (e.g., How long does one go to school to become a lawyer? How many women are lawyers? How much money does an average airline mechanic make?) As each question is raised, the teacher will ask if someone in the class would be able to get the answer. (e.g., who knows a lawyer well enough to ask?) The class, with their parents and friends, constitute a vast resource pool. Some questions, of course, may have to be assigned for library or telephone research.

4. Students should be encouraged to check out with teachers, counselors, or others, any feedback about their personal qualities which they disagree with and/or are concerned to know more about.

5. The final minutes should be used to allow students to share reactions to the exercise and to set a date on which answers to the assigned questions will be expected.

Want Ads

Objectives For Students:

1. To analyze in greater depth an occupation preferred on the DIVISRA.
2. To learn factors to consider about occupations (training and educational requirements, opportunities for advancement, working conditions, etc.).
3. To expand their perceptions to see the wide variety of jobs within areas of interest only indicated by one occupation on the DIVISRA.

Objectives For Teachers:

1. To have posters prepared for Exercise 21 which list a variety of want ads for the various occupations on the DIVISRA for the Job Hunting exercise which follows.

Time Required:

50 minutes (can be done as a homework assignment)

Number Of Participants:

Students may work individually or in pairs.

Materials:

1. Want ads from several different newspapers and professional journals. (Librarians or State Employment personnel can provide a list of names and addresses to contact for securing notices of advertised jobs—American Association of Nurses, Trade Union journals, APA Monitor, etc.)
2. Large sheets of newsprint, scissors, and paste.
3. Occupational Analysis Sheet (see step 3).

Process:

1. Each student will sign up to analyze the want ads for one of the jobs he/she responded to on the DIVISRA as one they would like to do. The teacher should devise some procedure to avoid unnecessary duplication and provide as wide coverage as possible.
2. Students will cut and paste want ads on as wide a variety as possible of jobs related to their choice, for example.

NURSE—A trained person who follows the doctor's directions in caring for sick persons, or helping them to stay well.

119

3. Each student will be given an occupational analysis sheet and instructed to study the want ads, collecting and recording the following information to add to his/her poster:

REPAIRER/INSTALLER—A person who fixes and puts in the machines and objects that we use, like TVs, Telephones and disposals.

OCCUPATIONAL ANALYSIS SHEET

1. What personal qualities seem to be necessary for this job?

Intellectual: _____

Physical: _____

Personality: _____

   a. Does this job seem to imply that one sex is preferred?
      Yes _____ No _____
      Why? _____

2. Write in any special requirements for this job or occupational area.

Education/training _____

Experience _____

Others _____

3. What are some of the working conditions stated by Employers? (e.g., night hours; travel; etc.)

_____

_____

4. How many different kinds of jobs were advertised within this occupational area? _____
(Cut out one of each kind.)

5. How many openings totally did you find advertised? _____

---

4. Students are encouraged to share their reactions to this exercise and be informed that they will get a chance to study each other's posters when they are placed around the room for the Job Hunting exercise.

Job Hunting

Objectives For Students:
1. To analyze attitudes and expand knowledge about particular vocational perception patterns: locked out, locked in, and least preferred.

Time Required:
50 minutes

Number Of Participants:
Maximum 60 students

Materials:
1. Each student will need his/her own response sheets from the DIVISRA.
2. Want ad posters for each job or occupational area of the DIVISRA should have been posted in a room large enough for students to mill around and study the posters.

Process:
1. The teacher will introduce the exercise; that is "we will explore occupa-

tional areas that you think you would enjoy, but view yourselves locked out of due to sex". Ask each student to look over their response blanks and identify which jobs have that particular pattern for them. Students may write them in a list if they prefer.

2. The teacher should lead a discussion which encourages students to extend the meaning of the particular pattern into the world of work both now and in the future. Students should try to examine the consequences for both sexes if attitudes remain the same.

   Locked Out—Pilot is a job that most of you girls see as one you'd enjoy but that men can best perform it. Why is that? Can you visualize this changing? What would have to happen in order to change the perceptions of students about this job?

3. Students will then be instructed to "mill about" the room studying the want ads of the particular jobs for which they have responded in this way until they find one that they could see themselves doing for at least some period in their lives. Students should make a mental note of what the factors are which caused them to change their mind.

4. After 20 minutes the students should be asked to stop and form into groups of eight or ten. In each group every student should have a chance to share their reactions; including those who are still "unemployed."

5. After 30 minutes, the class should meet as a total group and share their reactions to this exercise.

Note:

   This same exercise can be done two more times if the teacher has students deal with attitudes as defined below.

   "Locked IN" — I would *not* like to do this job but it falls to the members of my sex.

   Girl's pattern 😟 🧍‍♀️   Boy's pattern 😟 🧍

   "Least Preferred." I would not like this job at all. 😣

Planning Ahead

Objectives For Students:
1. To sensitize students to the problems which occur when they depart from traditional stereotypes in vocational planning and curriculum experiences.
2. To consider alternatives to dilemmas presented by these changes in terms of thoughtful planning of life style.

Time Required:
50 minutes for each role-playing situation.

Number Of Participants:
Open

Materials:
Ditto copies of "Departure Dilemmas." (Follows process)

Process:
1. The teacher asks for volunteers from the class and describes what "role

playing" means and how it can help the class to see the ways in which people react. That is, we frequently act according to the stereotypes we maintain rather than to the actual demands of people and situations. The teacher says: "The volunteers are offering to take the parts of characters in scenes they will be given. They will make up the action and the dialogue as they go along according to how they imagine the character they are playing would react in the situation."

2. After soliciting the proper number of volunteers for each of the Departure Dilemmas, the teacher will read the description of the scene to the entire group of students. The students are then given a minute to select roles and the scenes begin. Each of the Dilemmas has two scenes. No more than 15 minutes should be used to role play each.

3. Following the role-played situations the entire class is asked to react to the presentation in terms of accuracy of presentation, evidence of stereotyping in mannerisms, dialogue, and resolution of the situation. About 20 minutes should be allowed for this.

DEPARTURE DILEMMAS

1. Subject selection*

    a. We need four volunteers.
    b. Read: Bill (Carol) has the highest grades of any student in sixth grade. He has a keen interest in science, math, and electronics. He and his parents are trying to decide if Bill should enter the vocational junior high and if not, what subjects he should take in junior high school. Bill would like very much to go to medical school. His parents do not have much money and he knows that this would require them to make a lot of sacrifices for a long time while he went to college. Bill is also interested in pursuing a career in computers and electronics and if he attended vocational secondary schools he could get a job right out of high school.
    c. (1) Bill (Carol) is meeting with a school counselor.
       (2) Bill (Carol) is meeting with school counselor without parents.

2. Girls spoil all the fun.

    a. First we need eight volunteers and then we'll need four more.
    b. Read: Glenda has signed up for metal shop and graphics at Sunshine

*Use whichever sex you prefer, Bill or Carol.

Junior High although these classes have always been composed of boys in the past. When she begins the classes she finds that the boys are hostile and no boy will work with her on any project. They complain about having a girl in the class openly to the teacher. Glenda's girlfriends have been giving her a bad time as well.

c. (1) Glenda in the class with teacher and five boys.

    (2) Glenda walking home with four of her girlfriends.

3. Why should they have to?

a. We need six volunteers for the first situation and six for the second.

b. Read: The parents of many boys attending Traditional Junior High strongly object to the new regulation that all boys must take one year of home economics. In the past the curriculum has been cooking, sewing, good appearance and poise, home decoration and repairs, budgeting, and infant and child care.

c. (1) Four parents from PTA are meeting with the teacher and principal to make suggestions for re-designing the course. Two of the parents object to boys having to take the course.

    (2) Four students are meeting with the teacher and principal to make suggestions for re-designing the course. Two of the students are girls and two are boys.

4. Our masculinity is at stake.

a. We need five volunteers for the first situation and six volunteers for the second situation.

b. Read: At Desperado Junior High the TWO female and FOUR male intramural baseball teams meet and play competitively after school. However, the girls' teams are racking up an impressive number of wins over the boys, and the boys are dismayed. The physical education faculty has concluded that the situation occurred because only the highly motivated girls came out for intramurals, while the more athletic boys did not elect baseball.

c. (1) The two female and two male physical education teachers are meeting to decide what to do about the situation.

    (2) One representative from each of the boys' teams is meeting with two representatives from the girls' teams to decide what they should do about the situation.

Is That Me In The Future?

Objectives For Students:

1. To give students a chance to project their concerns regarding departures from traditional sex-roles into the future in order to consider feelings and ways to manage feelings.
2. To become sensitized to viewing a vocation as one facet of the person which plays a part in the total life style of that person.

Time Required:

Open

Materials:

Some situations are provided for role playing at end of the exercise. However, the teacher will want to create situations from questions and concerns posed by students from their work in previous vocational exercises. Most especially should situations which students present for ridicule (e.g., male at home while wife works) be used and carried through in a serious vein.

Process:

1. The teacher should explain to the students that role playing sensitizes

people to the stereotypes we share about men, women, parents, workers, etc. Role playing also provides us with a means to project into the future; anticipating possible consequences and giving us needed practice in managing alternatives. The teacher will further explain that students will be asked to volunteer to role play various situations and describe the role play various situations and describe the role playing process: "The volunteers will be offering to take the parts of characters in scenes they will be given. They will make up the action and the dialogue as they go along according to how they imagine the character they are playing would react in the situation."

2. The teacher, after securing the proper number of volunteers for each situation, reads the description of the scene to the entire group of students. The students assign themselves the roles within the situation and the scene begins. The teacher may ask them to reverse roles in the middle of role playing if things seem to hit a snag.

3. Following each role-playing situation the entire group should be asked to react to the presentation in terms of accuracy of presentation, evidence of stereotyping in mannerisms, dialogue, resolution of the situation, etc.

SAMPLES OF ROLE-PLAYING SITUATIONS

1. WHAT'S the matter with Johnny?

    a. We need two volunteers.

    b. Read: In a home the female pilot is discussing plans to re-decorate the home and a problem with one of the two children with her husband. Johnny, it seems, is throwing rocks and hits the children in the neighborhood. The husband is a free-lance artist who works at home five hours each day while a neighbor keeps the children. He carries most of the home responsibilities, particularly while his wife is away on a long flight.

    c. Role play the above situation. Allow twelve minutes.

    d. Total group reaction to the role playing. Allow fifteen minutes.

---

2. WHO gets the business?

    a. We need three volunteers.

    b. Read: A male owner and manager of the Hire-A-Maid Corporation is interviewing two applicants for one job opening. Unemployment is high and both persons need the job badly to support their families. One applicant is a male and one is a female.

c. Role play the above situation. Allow fifteen minutes.

d. Total group reaction to the role playing. Allow 15-20 minutes.

---

3. WHO'S the boss?

    a. We need two volunteers.

    b. Read: A female police lieutenant is meeting with one of her patrol officers to discuss his performance. He does some things very well but there are two areas he needs to improve on: punctuality and getting reports written and in. He is interested in a promotion which is soon to be open and he needs her recommendation.

    c. Role play the above situation. Allow ten minutes.

    d. Total group reaction to the role playing. Allow fifteen minutes.

---

4. WHO should get the job?

    a. We need five volunteers.

    b. Read: A principal and three teachers are interviewing a male for the position of school nurse. If he gets the job he will also be asked to teach health and hygiene courses to boys and girls.

    c. Role play the above situation. Allow fifteen minutes.

    d. Total group reaction to role playing. Allow fifteen minutes.

Do Our Textbooks Expand Our Dreams?

Objectives For Students:
1. To collect empirical evidence on role images.
2. To share results of collections.
3. To compare and interpret results.
4. To compare results with reality.
5. To hypothesize about how to eliminate negative results found.

Time Required:
2 class periods of 50 minutes

Number Of Participants:
Open

Materials:
1. Students' textbooks
2. Ditto copies of survey and pencils
3. Newsprint and magic markers

Process:
1. Students will be asked to select two or three of their textbooks for analysis.

2. Copies of the text survey are distributed to students and the teacher will give instructions.
3. Results will be tabulated on newsprint for each subject area separately.
4. Students will discuss the results comparing facts about texts with facts in the world about them.

SURVEY

Title of Text _____

Subject Area _____

Pictures: How many _____   Number of boys/men _____
                                 Number of girls/women _____

Pictures portray:

_____ Active _____   _____ Passive _____

____ men/boys   ____ women/girls   ____ men/boys   ____ women/girls

Vocations portrayed (list):
(Use the back if needed.)

Men/Boys   Women/Girls

_____   _____

_____   _____

_____   _____

_____   _____

Comments about the written text material:

_____

_____

_____

_____

_____

_____

_____

_____

_____

25

101 Quick Ways To Promote Feeling Expression And Acceptability While Eliminating Boy-Girl Lines

Objectives For Students:
1. To identify and concretize their feelings.
2. To own their feelings and develop increased awareness of their responsibility for their feelings.
3. To become aware that they are not alone in their feelings.
4. To be encouraged to express and act on feelings in positive ways.
5. To develop greater empathy for others.
6. To become aware of the multitude of human feelings at conceptual level.

Objectives For Teachers:
1. To develop an ongoing awareness of the affective state of students for planning and student guidance.

Process:

In order to act wisely on our feelings we must learn appropriate labels for the myriad of feelings humans are heir to; we must also come to recognize accurately and accept our vast storehouse of feelings and somehow find socially acceptable ways to share their wealth with others. (Conceptualize, recognize, express, and exchange.)

It is the intent of the following brief activities to help students achieve just such learnings and achieve them in what has heretofore been unused time—transition time; the time used to get from one activity to another and from one place to another in a school building. All of the activities assume double lines, designated "Here," "There." But the creative teacher will have little difficulty modifying them to her purposes; e.g., "First," "Second."

The activities themselves are presented in the following order: those which primarily deal with a conceptual understanding of feelings; those which encourage expression of feelings; and those which encourage students to act on their feeling. This is done because it is usually easier for students and teachers to begin at the cognitive level but as soon as students show readiness it is wise to move to the other levels and thereafter back and forth. Ideally, the teacher and students will soon be creating their own activities out of their own experience.

Conceptual Level

Call to Line Up

A. *Feelings have various shades and degrees.*
Everyone who can think of a word that means almost the same thing as *love* line up HERE. And everyone who can think of a feeling like love but not as strong line up THERE.

Sharing

Call on a few people to say their word(s) aloud or let each person whisper his word to the person next to them in line.

(It rarely happens that a child is unable to get into line, but if this occurs the teacher will exercise creativity; e.g., "You may go up and down the line and let each person whisper theirs to you. Get into line beside someone who has a word you plan to remember, or like."

Creating More of Your Own

Only ten feeling words are given below. Use of Roget's Thesaurus can expand the number of line-up occasions into the hundreds.

HERE   1. *Love* words—affection, fond, adore, attachment, passion.

THERE   *Positive attraction* words—like, regard, fancy, admire, relish, esteem.

        2. *Hate* words—despise, abhor, abominate, detest, loathe.

        Less than words—vexed, irritated, annoyed, offended.

        3. *Happy* words—cheerful, glad, gay, blithe, gleeful.

        More than words—ecstasy, joy, delight, thrilled, transported.

4. *Sad* words—unhappy, dejected, gloomy, grave.

   More than words—depressed, agonized, despondent, despairing, miserable.

5. *Angry or more than* words—vexed, exasperated, rage, seething, furious, wrathful, stormy.

   Angry or less than words—aggravated, irritated, annoyed, displeased.

6. *Fine* words (as in how are you?)—fit, sound, chipper, tolerable.

   Not fine words—ill, sick, morbid, diseased, infectious, down.

7. *Wonder* words—astound, awe, astonish, marvel, fascinate, surprise.

   Opposite of wonder words—cool, imperturbable, unsurprised, blase, calm.

8. *Anxious* words—uncertain, apprehensive, concerned, qualms, doubting.

   More than anxious words—frightened, panic stricken, dreading, phobic, terror-ridden, haunted, aghast, petrified.

9. *Contented* words—satisfied, complacent, peaceful, at ease, quiet.

   Opposite of Contented words—dissatisfied, discontented, out of temper, bad humor, glum, hypercritical, sore, disappointed, disturbed.

10. *Confident* words—assured, hopeful, fearless, reliable, trustworthy, sound, certain, resolute, bold.

    Opposite of confident words—fallible, vulnerable, uncertain, doubtful.

Call to Line Up

B. *Feelings can be described and put in words.*

11. Everyone who agrees with Shelley or knows what he means when he says: "Our sincerest laughter with some *pain* is fraught," line up HERE.

    Everyone who thinks pain induces callousness, line up THERE.

Sharing

Call one one or two persons to explain in each line. If anyone cannot identify with either line, ask them to state what they think a function of pain is.

Creating More of Your Own

Roget's Thesaurus can be consulted for more examples and/or students themselves encouraged to create one liners about emotion. (See numbers 13 through 17 below.)

HERE
THERE

12. *Grief* that's beauty's canker—Shakespeare
    Tears are the noble language of the Eye—Herrick

13. Beware the *fury* of a patient man—Dryden
    I prefer the fiery vehemence of youth—Scott

14. What can't be cured, must be *endured*.
    No one is a victim. If you don't like a thing, change it.

15. When *feeling* enters the front gate wisdom goes out the back.
    The advantage of emotions is that they lead us astray—O. Wilde

16. You can't demonstrate an emotion—Morley
    If you really *loved* me, you'd show it.

17. Every form of human life is *romantic*—T. Higginson
    Man is a wolf to man—Plautus

18. We are *cold* to others only when we are dull in ourselves—Hazlitt
    You cannot demonstrate an emotion—Morley

19. *Compassion* cures more sins than condemnation—H. W. Beecher
    Pity is not helpful to those who bear guilt.

20. *Laugh* and the world laughs with you. Weep and you weep alone—
    E. W. Wilcox
    Rejoice with them that do rejoice and weep with them that weep—
    Bible

21. *Pity* is the deadliest thing that can be offered to a woman—V. Baum
    A brother's sufferings claim a brother's pity—Addison

22. When I'm not thanked at all, I'm thanked enough—Fielding
    How sharper than a serpent's tooth it is to have a *thankless* child—
    Shakespeare

HERE   23. Describe *suffering* so that you can feel it. (e.g., "Suffering worked
    its way down to his/her stomach like ground glass.")

THERE   Describe suffering so that you can see it. (e.g., "Suffering folded her
    body with the weight of a hundred years.")

24. Describe *calm* so that you can see it.
    Describe calm so that you can feel it.

25. *Quiet* as seen.
    Quiet as felt.

26. *Angry* as tasted.
    Angry as smelled.

27. *Apprehensive* as felt.
    Apprehensive as tasted.

Call to Line Up

C. *Sometimes we have ambivalent feelings.*

28. Everyone who can think of words to describe positive feelings about parents' concern about who our friends are, line up HERE.

    Everyone who can think of words to describe some of the negative feelings we have about our parents' concerns about who our friends are, line up THERE.

Sharing

Call on a few students to role play the parent in such a way that the word is available for the rest of the class to guess.

Creating More of Your Own

At some time ask students in your class to list people, things, and places that cause them to feel ambivalent. Use this list in place of or along with those that follow.

HERE
THERE

29. Words that describe positive feelings toward young children or babies. Words that describe negative feelings toward young children or babies.

    (Be sure to call attention to the fact that both boys and girls line up for both kinds of feelings.)

30. Words that describe positive feelings toward horror movies; negative feelings.

31. Positive and negative feelings after a game.

32. Positive and negative feelings about a friend who tells you the truth about yourself when the truth is not complimentary.

33. Positive and negative feelings toward a teacher who gives you the exact grade you earned on your report card.

34. Positive and negative feelings toward a teacher who gives you a higher grade than you earned on your report card.

35. Toward a rainy day.

36. Toward the dawn.

37. Toward work.

Expressive Level

Call to Line Up

Everyone who has felt _____ (use any emotion) at least some-time [today, yesterday, this week], line up HERE. Those who haven't, line up THERE.

Everyone who wouldn't want to live in a world where they didn't ex-perience _____ (use any emotion) at least once [every three days, every day, ever], line up HERE. Everyone else line up THERE.

The time selected is dependent upon whether the emotion in question is more or less positive; if it's "negative," allow for greater distance from it—at least in initial work with students.

Sharing

Call on those who volunteer to share only in regard to the "positive" emotion words. Be quite direct as for your reason in doing this: "People can choose to stay with pleasant or unpleasant feelings just as many of us choose to feel the way we do by choosing to do things that we've learned will make us feel good. When we feel good we should dwell on it a little bit; savor it, take it in and most of us are not used to doing that."

When lining up deals with the "bad" or painful feelings sharing is best done by the teacher if he/she can do this before the line up is called. For example, with "Who has felt angry at least once today?" The teacher can express that he or she let this happen by planning more than could get done in the last period and then getting irritated with self be-cause "I should have known better, and I tend to get angry with myself when I'm not perfect." The teacher shares because the teacher goes on to explain how he/she took responsibility for getting self out of the feeling. Then when line up is called the sharing of one or two students is limited to how to be kind to self and avoid dwelling on or ruminating about the feeling.

Creating More of Your Own

Return to the list of emotions one through ten and/or use Roget's Thesaurus, or the fifteen words below.

38—67 (minimum). Use the following fifteen words in the two sen-tences above.

joy	glum	thrilled
furious	satisfied	guilty
awe	disappointed	hopeful
panic	cheerful	embarrassed
fascination	shocked	contented

68. Those who can think of two things that make them feel good about themselves, line up HERE, and those who can only think of one thing, line up THERE.

69. Those who can think of two things which make you feel pain, line up HERE, and those who can only think of one thing line up THERE.

70. Who had an exciting lovely thought today? Line up HERE. Those who would like to hear one line up THERE.

71. Those who just had a feeling come over them sometime today, line up HERE. Those who are responsible for a feeling they felt today, line up THERE.

Action Level

72. Those who know how many pleasant things happened to them yesterday, line up HERE. Those who never bothered to keep count, line up THERE.

73. Those who have not found a way to discipline themselves for one self-indulgent habit such as eating, skipping homework or losing temper, line up HERE. Those who think they have discovered a way that works at least part of the time line up THERE. (Call on volunteers in the THERE line to share their secrets.)

74. Those who are having a wonderful time with their lives this week, line up HERE. Those who think it could be better, line up THERE. Then we'll give you a break and let you go first.

75. Everyone who has discovered at least one way to make themselves happy, line up over HERE. Those who would like to learn at least one more way to make yourselves happy, line up THERE. Find someone in the other line and share for a minute.

76. Those who think they are responsible for their own feelings, line up HERE. Those who think they aren't, line up THERE. Choose one person in the other line and exchange reasons for one minute.

77. Everyone who has discovered one way they make themselves unhappy, line up HERE. Everyone who has found one way that other people make them unhappy, line up THERE. Choose a partner from

the other line and each listen to each other and try to suggest a solution in the next two minutes. If you can't shake hands or hug each other—misery loves company.

78. Everyone who had a painful moment yesterday or today line up HERE. Everyone who didn't line up THERE. Choose a partner from the painful line and supply a non-verbal symbolic band aid.

For 79 through 85

Those who did something that they are proud of yesterday, line up HERE. Those who can't think of anything, line up THERE and we'll give you a direction which you can follow so you'll feel that way before the day is over.

79. Make a child feel more worthwhile by really listening to what he/she has to say for five minutes.

80. Give someone a genuine compliment.

81. Eat something that is good for you.

82. Take on a slightly tough challenge and pat yourself on the back for your courage whether you fail or not.

83. Catch yourself when you're getting irritated and walk away for a minute and ask yourself, is it worth it; even if you have to do it mentally.

84. Find something beautiful and gaze at it for a while.

85. Think of one thing you can do that is being kind to yourself and that won't make you feel guilty later.

86. Those who have something to do that they want to avoid doing but know they will feel bad if they avoid it, line up over HERE. Those who have a bit of a need to be bossy today, line up over THERE. Choose someone in the avoiding line and tell them to do It.

For 87 through 101

Building concrete mental images.

One minute before you call lines, ask students to try to form a visual image of themselves as _____ (see emotions 88-101). Encourage this image building process by asking them what the facial expression is? What the image is doing? etc. Then call lines by those who have an image, line up HERE; and those who can't come up with a visual image, line up THERE. Let those with a visual image share it with the others either verbally or nonverbally through pantomime. Work through the eight positive images first and then the seven childish sin images. For each of the seven childish sin images have students use their image process a bit further, calling mentally on their compassionate humane image (No. 94) to come to the child image, take the child's hand and explain what to do. Students are usually surprised at how much easier it is to come up with a visual image for the seven childish sins. It is helpful if the teacher starts off the imagining for the seven childish sins by presenting a few ideas (ideas which keep the images within bounds and out of candidacy for horror movies). As an example for the furious child image, the teacher can suggest a child lying on the floor kicking his/her heels or a child facing people with a pop-gun of the "Peter and the Wolf" variety.

87. Those who have now a mental image of themselves as strong and assertive, standing for what they believe in, line up HERE. Those who can't yet get a picture, line up THERE while we share images to get you started so you can go on working on it till one comes to you.

88. gracious

89. loving

90. cheerful

91. conscientious

92. appreciative

93. contented

94. compassionate and humane

95. self-indulgent

96. angry

97. sloppy

98. staller

99. whiner

100. complainer

101. negative and contrary

The Educatory And Parents: Introduction

This section provides exercises for parents and teachers of students, grades kindergarten through eight. However, if the orientation of the school program for grades seven and eight is more secondary than middle school, the exercises in Volume Two might be more appropriate for educators and parents.

Each exercise, whether for teacher or parent, has three basic purposes underlying the objectives: (1) to build individual and group awareness of knowledge and attitudes about sex-roles through a self-assessment process; (2) to acquire additional information about cultural sex-stereotyping and alternatives to same; and (3) to plan actions on the basis of one and two for the purposes of furthering student growth.

One basic distinction relative to the sex-stereotyping that occurs in the lives of the younger students addressed by this volume is that basic academic experiences are open to both sexes; that is, subject selection and/or tracking characteristic of the older years it's not yet present. In this respect, there is less opportunity for restriction of sex roles. That which does occur is usually related to teacher style and teaching techniques governed by attitudes and lack of awareness. The exercises for educators focus on these. Due to the fact that parents have a dominant influence on the sex-role preferences of their children, two exercises for parents dealing with this topic have been included in this section.

In exercise 26 school situations are presented which provide an opportunity for reinforcement of traditional sex-stereotypes or for expanding beyond sex-role restrictions. The participants are asked to choose that response which most nearly represents their individual behavior preference. One result, in addition to allowing participants to assess their own tendencies, is that they are stimulated to examine sex-stereotyping in specific areas of the education process—physical education,

working with parents, child development, assumptions about personal-social behavior, and intellect. Following the assessment portion of the exercise are small
group discussions on the same topics. Participants are then engaged in a needs
assessment where they select the areas they consider important for further exploration and activities. Such processes as accepting participants' current attitudes;
questioning them to look further; encouraging them to exchange viewpoints in
peer groups; and allowing them to help chart their own course, are fundamental to
laying groundwork for attitude change.

Exercise 27 presents participants with six student case examples. In one, a
student is sent to office for disciplinary action; in another a student wants to avoid
school as a way of handling fears. Participants are asked to choose solutions, una-
ware that an equal number of their fellow participants have the same case example
but labeled with identification data of the opposite sex. The solutions chosen are
then tabulated by the group to discover how gender alters treatment. Participants
quickly discover that differences do exist; that the boy is generally accorded a different type of discipline than the girl, that boys are in general helped to deal with
their fears in different fashion, etc. Meaningful discussion follows as to why, and
the implications and consequences of sex-differential treatment. The learnings
thus acquired are less easily forgotten than facts from a lecture or film. That is
not to say that information is never introduced in such in-service training, but like
most things it is a question of timing. Participants are eager to hear, view, and read
further about the validity of their own workshop learnings.

Certainly, the trainer and participants for each activity need to be familiar
with up to date research about sex differential treatment and cognitive development—the latter never to be considered an isolated unfolding process from the
network of interpersonal relationships.

1. Generally boys need less aggression and more impulse control than they
normally have, to facilitate intellectual achievement, while girls need greater im-
pulsivity and aggression than they normally have for optimum intellectual achievement.*

2. Girls have a better initial start on cognitive development than boys; they
say first words earlier; they combine words into sentences sooner; and they count
accurately sooner than boys. In the early school years, boys have more reading
problems and learn to read later than girls. After fifth or sixth grade, girls continue to excell in punctuation, verbal fluency, and spelling, although boys have
caught up in comprehension by this time. In mathematics, the sexes do not differ
significantly in early or middle school years; however, by college boys have forged

*Maccoby, Eleanor E. "Woman's Intellect" in S. M. Farber and R. H. L. Wilson (Eds.), *Potential of Women*,
New York; McGraw-Hill, 1963.
Sutton-Smith, B. Roberts, J. W. and Rosenberg, B. G. "Sibling Associations and Role Involvement," Merrill-
Palmer Quarterly, 1964, 10, 25-38.
Kagan, Jerome and Moss, Howard, *Birth To Maturity*, New York; Wiley, 1962.
Sigel, I. E., Jarman, P. and Hanesian, H. "Styles of Categorization and Their Perceptual, Intellectual and
Personality Correlates in Young Children," Merrill-Palmer Institute, Detroit, Michigan, 1963.

much farther ahead than girls. Research strongly indicates that the differences discussed above are strongly influenced by the teaching of socialization of sex roles and related patterns of child rearing.

3. The methods of child rearing which encourage passivity and dependence such as those generally employed with girls have the same effects whether they are used on girls or boys. They result in lower achievement and intellectual accomplishments overall and lead to good performance in subjects like language and spelling, which depend on rules.

> "However, a conformist upbringing snuffs out the twin candles
> of curiosity and creativity that burn in young children's minds."
> (Rogers, 1969a)   p. 263

What does all this mean to the educator in terms of appropriate treatment of both sexes? Educators can help parents to become aware of what sex-stereotyping is and what effects it has on their child's development since parents play a dominant role in that development in the years before adolescence. Exercises 29 and 30 are included for this purpose. Beyond that, and on a daily basis with the students, educators must compensate for the sex-stereotyping acquired in the non-school world and in previous development. The weight of the research points to "ideal" cognitive development as one which combines the "masculine" traits of curiosity, energy, self-confidence, activity, and resistance to conformity, with the "feminine" traits of warmth and sensitivity for either sex student.

Exercise 27 continues the process of helping teachers recognize possible individual sex-biases by asking participants to examine their student preference. The analyses of most and least preferred student characteristics is carried out relative to sex. One frequent outcome which often surprises participants is that "most preferred male students" usually have characteristics common to both sexes' stereotypes, while "most preferred female students" reflect only traditional female stereotypes.

Another important outcome of exercise 27 is that it helps participants better understand the emotional needs of their "least preferred students."

Exercise 28 accents the theme of emotional needs of adolescence by presenting teachers with a common story telling and creative writing experience concerning what students did during a summer vacation. The purpose of the exercise is to help teachers acquire greater skill in recognizing dominant emotional themes of students as they relate personal experiences of how this recognition of emotional themes is influenced by the sex of students. Again, the instructor has a chance to assess individual biases and those of his/her professional peer group in dealing with understanding the students they teach.

The last two exercises, numbers 29 and 30, are for parents. They invite the parent to examine the issue of sex-stereotyping in a career education context on a personal basis involving their own children. The parents are asked, through quick paper and pencil assessment, to identify for themselves whether they possess chauvinistic tendencies. Preaching is not done regarding "shoulds" or "should nots" but after the self-assessment and small group discussion, factual data from Bureau of Labor Statistics is presented for the parent to draw his/her own conclusions. For example, the parent who takes the position, "I'm going to protect my little girl from the harsh realities of this world until I hand her over to a husband who will do likewise," has to examine this position in the light of the harsh realities reflected by divorce statistics, widowhood, the lower skill level and educational preparation of women which still exists today. Many parents have reported loosening their grip concerning long held attitudes of sex-role stereotyping after participating in these exercises.

26

Testing Your Sexual Democracy Quotient Through Hypothetical School Situations: Level I

Objectives For Educators:

1. To evaluate their individual preferences for behaviors which reinforce or encourage departure from sex-role stereotyping in education.
2. To identify specific behaviors and educational procedures which are sex-biased.
3. To analyze the following areas relative to sex-bias and sex-role stereo-typing: physical education and athletics, school facilities, texts and instructional materials, psychology of student development, behavior and motivation, educational legislation, career aspirations, parent pressure, and administrative opportunities.

Objectives For Workship Trainer/Facilitators:

1. To assess participants educational needs and interests for further workshop planning.

Time Required:

2 hours

Number Of Participants:

Minimum of 10

Materials:

One copy for each participant of: "Educational Procedures and Student Behavior Management: Elementary Form," Scoring Key for same, and answer blanks.

Process:

1. The facilitator/trainer explains the purpose of the exercise and tells each participant that they will be scoring their own responses.

2. Copies of the "Educational Procedures and Student Behavior Management" and answer blanks are distributed to each participant. They are instructed to read directions and answer on separate blanks in 15 minutes.

3. Scoring Keys are distributed and participants are given instructions for scoring. When scoring is completed, they are asked to keep the test and Scoring Key for discussion in small groups, at which time they will be collected. They are asked to record their score anonymously on a slip of paper. These slips are collected and the trainer tallies and plots the entire group's range during the following step.

4. Participants form small groups of 8–10 and choose a leader to facilitate the discussion and report the group's conclusions. Participants are first encouraged to discuss any of the items of interest or scoring of contention. Then each small group receives one of the following topic areas:

   a. Do teachers give rewards (praise, positive attention, etc.) and punishments differentially to male and female students? In a survey, teachers and administrators report that males are asked more questions and that teaching is geared more to males. Do you think this is true? If so, why?

   b. Which are true sex differences and which are myths? Include personality variables, interests, and abilities in your discussion.

   c. Although some progress has been made, textbooks and instructional media are heavily sex-stereotyped. The extent to which this is true has been thoroughly verified through research. However, some educators argue that no research has been done which reveals it has any effect on student behavior and that in fact other factors are far more important. Do you agree or disagree? Give reasons.

   d. Does the almost total male dominance in school leadership contribute to sex-role stereotyping in schools?

   e. Can legislation remove sex-bias from schools?

   f. How can teachers counteract the fact that boys and girls have been conditioned to have very real sex-related interests (through previously acquired sex-stereotypes) without letting them make choices on basis of interest or building the curriculum on the basis of interest and motivation. Should they take affirmative action? If so, how? (For example, if girls would rather read romance stories and boys science fiction; if girls aren't interested in electronics and boys aren't interested in typing).

   g. What are valid criteria, if any, for grouping by sex for physical education or health education?

5. The large group reassembles and each small group leader is asked to report out the main points of the group's discussion and conclusions, if any. Two or three questions, comments or reactions from the entire group should follow each small group report.

6. On newsprint (or by individual ballot) the group is tallied as to what areas they consider most important to pursue further. The trainer honors this priority listing in future planning.

   Example: Please indicate 3 areas of sexual democracy you believe are most important for educator involvement.

     ☐ Self-awareness activities/consciousness-raising

     ☐ Analyses of textbooks and instructional media

     ☐ Legal issues and sex equality

     ☐ Physical education, health education

     ☐ Psychology of males and females

     ☐ Women's studies, women in history, etc.

     ☐ Women, men, and administrative positions

     ☐ Broadening career opportunities

     ☐ Planning sex-equal curriculum

     ☐ Other: (Please write in)

     ☐ Other: (Please write in)

7. The range of scores with tallies is posted so that individuals may compare without disclosing their score to their peers.

EDUCATIONAL PROCEDURES AND STUDENT BEHAVIOR MANAGEMENT: ELEMENTARY FORM

Directions: One elementary school situation is described in each of the 10 items which follow. Study each situation and select the *one* answer you think best on the basis of what is presented or implied in the item situation.

1. The boys and girls in Sunshine Elementary have gym together every day. The parents and teachers of the school would like to begin a program of having wrestling and karate for the boys and modern dance for the girls every Friday.

   What should be done?

   a. They should do it. Integrated gym classes four out of five days is sufficient evidence of a commitment to the goal of sexual democracy in physical education.
   b. They should offer the two choices on Fridays but permit students to sign up regardless of sex.
   c. They should not separate the students but instead give both offerings on separate days to all students.
   d. They should offer gymnastics to all on Friday instead.

2. A bill has been introduced to the Senate which seeks to eliminate certain provisions currently called for under Title IX. Assume that you are contacting your Senator and expressing your beliefs about what portions should be eliminated. Read each of the numbered suggestions below:

   1. Eliminate the provisions which enable women to have easier access to administrative positions.
   2. Retain the portions which forbid sex discrimination in educational programs but eliminate portions which relate to physical education or athletics.
   3. Retain the portions which forbid sex discrimination in educational programs but eliminate portions which relate to extracurricular activities.
   4. Eliminate Title IX entirely. The Civil Rights Act can be made to apply to all important aspects of discrimination.

   Now choose from a, b, c, or d what you would recommend:

   a. I would recommend none of the above.
   b. I would recommend (1) only.
   c. I would recommend (2) and (3) only.
   d. I would recommend (4).

3. You are concerned about eliminating sex-role stereotyping in your classroom and you are also interested in allowing children to make their own decisions and develop their own individual interests. But during free choice time on the playground or in the classroom, the boys play football and inside get out the toy trucks, while the girls jump rope or play house outside and inside they go to the doll corner.

   What should you do?

   a. Eliminate the doll corner and discourage the girls' playing house by telling them that almost all of them will take a job outside the

148

house at some time in their lives.

b. Encourage broader sports participation by getting the girls into the team games.

c. When it is not free time, introduce and organize play activities which are non-sex stereotyped and randomly select students for participation regardless of sex.

d. Nothing; children's use of free play reflects their attempt to adapt to culture and should not be interfered with.

4. While more than two-thirds of elementary and secondary school teachers are women, only about 15% of the principals and only about one-half of 1% of superintendents are women.

What do these statistics really mean?

a. Women do not possess the desire to become administrators. Most female teachers have families and do not want the heavy responsibility.

b. Women do not possess the competencies for administrative positions. Their skills are more nuturant and valuable for fostering student development in the classroom.

c. Women are discriminated against regarding promotions in education.

d. Women are reluctant to work for other women.

5. A group of teachers at Traditional Elementary have demanded that the school librarian refuse to order books which have been listed by several nationally known women's movement groups as sex-biased. The librarian fears the implementation of censorship over purchasing reading material.

What should be done?

a. Comply, only after a determination by a panel of experts on sex-stereotyping have read the books and agreed that they are in fact sex-biased.

b. Set up new ordering procedures which include the provision that if a percentage of teachers and/or students request a book it gets on the purchasing list regardless of sex-bias.

c. Comply and do not order the books because the school has an obligation to help students expand their perceptions of the roles of each sex.

d. Refuse to alter purchasing procedures on the basis of whether a book is sex-biased.

6. At a faculty meeting a school psychologist says that most behavior problems are boys because most teachers are women and they tend to reward docile conforming behavior. Since most boys are not socialized that way, they tend to be classroom problems. In the discussion which follows each teacher is asked to respond with comments and suggestions.

Which of the following would be nearest your response?

   a. I would like us to plan someway, perhaps in service training, to help teachers learn other ways of managing boys who present problem behavior.

   b. I think rewarding this behavior which enable students to follow directions and attend to learning is valid and necessary. If boys are not taught this in the rest of our culture it is especially important that they learn it at school.

   c. Then, let us explore the possibilities of insuring a boy with at least one male classroom teacher during his elementary school years.

   d. Let us provide separate educational activities for those who need to explode within boundaries and other activities for those who need to be less docile and conforming.

7. Children in several fifth grade classes were told the following story:

A boy and girl who lived near each other and had grown up friends decided to cooperate on a very difficult project for the Science Fair. They both worked equally as hard at planning and building the project. They worked many long hard hours after school for a month before the project was finished. Their hard work paid off and they won first prize in the state. They both had their pictures in the paper and TV. There was only one problem: First prize included a plane ticket to the World Science Fair and there was only one ticket and not enough time to raise money for another ticket.

Who should get the ticket?

1. The boy should go because he probably worked harder.
2. The girl should go because it takes more effort for a girl to succeed in science.
3. The girl should go because girls need more reinforcement to remain in the science field.
4. The girl should go because there will be many more opportunities available to boys in the future.
5. The girls should go as a matter of courtesy and good manners.

Which answer(s) from above would you consider acceptable?

   a. One only
   b. Five only
   c. Two, three and four
   d. None

8. Several parents recognizing that most boys mature more slowly than girls wish to keep their sons in Kindergarten an extra year so that they will do better in school.

Which do you think is the best basic policy for the schools to adopt when they receive such requests? (recognizing, of course, that no policy is totally rigid.)

a. A refusal on the basis that two years of undemanding academics tends to encourage attitudes that school is a play place which is even more dangerous for boys than girls.

b. No, because this only furthers the discrimination that already exists against boys in the elementary schools. Teachers and schools need to consider changing their methods.

c. Refusal, because this begins a dangerous policy which permits males to get a larger share of the school tax dollar.

d. Refusal on the basis that boys' abilities allow them to catch up and even surpass girls in the secondary schools and honoring such requests would only widen the gap.

9. Students from the third grade visited a local children's TV show. They were asked to line up and as each passed the microphone, tell what they wanted to be when they grew up. The girls' answers were teacher, nurse, secretary, and beautician except for one girl who said veternarian. The boys answers were much broader, but the main ones were fireman, policeman, doctor, President, and engineer.

Which of the following would you recommend for curriculum follow-up?

a. Have students engage in activities (reading, guest speakers, field trips, and discussion) which provide information about the above jobs as a background for more realistic choice later on.

b. Follow-up is unnecessary since even the research reveals that vocational choices at this age are unrealistic. Time would be more valuably expended on the basics which are necessary to all vocations.

c. Provide activities and information as vocations are relevant to the units of study in third grade, with emphasis on the fact that men or women can fill these jobs.

d. Plan a unit on vocations and involve boys and girls in role try-on experiences that deliberately reverses the traditional occupational roles; e.g. boys as nurses and telephone operators and girls as construction workers and mechanics.

10. American Elementary is an older school with separate bathroom facilities for boys and girls in the hall corridors at each end of its two wings. Due to its large enrollment special times have been assigned to each class for bathroom use. Students go from place to place in the building in lines (cafeteria, library, dismissal doors) and since the bathrooms are one of these places, teachers have traditionally had their students form a girls'

line and a boys' line for all class movements in the building. Some teachers are anxious to avoid sex-stereotyping yet they don't know what to do about this tradition which is so familiar to all the students.

What do you recommend?

a. Have the children line up by some other criteria than sex except when going to the bathroom.
b. Remain with the traditional way; it's too confusing to line up differently for different purposes and separate lines do not constitute sex-discrimination any more than the basic biological facts that call for separate bathrooms.
c. Have only one line and let children separate at the bathrooms.
d. Do away with concept of separate sex bathrooms.

SCORING KEY FOR EDUCATIONAL PROCEDURES AND STUDENT BEHAVIOR MANAGEMENT: ELEMENTARY FORM

1	1	3	4	3	Reinforcing traditional stereotypes: physical education and parent pressure
2	4	0	1	0	Title IX
3	4	3	3	1	Encouraging non-traditional career aspirations
4	0	0	3	0	Women as educational administrators
5	3	2	4	0	Censorship and sex-bias in educational media
6	1	1	1	3	Reinforcing personality stereotypes and disciplinary procedures
7	0	0	2	2	Student evaluation or merit
8	1	3	1	0	Differential abilities of males and females
9	2	1	3	4	Vocational aspirations
10	3	0	3	4	Educational techniques

0 = Practice *very much* reinforces traditional sex-role stereotypes.

1 = Practice *somewhat* reinforces traditional sex-role stereotypes.

2 = Practice is *neutral* as regards sex-role stereotyping.

3 = Practice encourages *some* departure from sex-role stereotypes.

4 = Practice *very much* encourages departure from sex-role stereotypes.

How Do I Treat Thee?
Level I

Objectives For Educators:
1. To problem solve case examples of particular students for growth producing outcomes.
2. To assess the extent to which educators' individual decisions compare to traditional sex-stereotyped solutions.
3. To evaluate group tendencies for growth producing outcome to be biased by sex of student: i.e., are girls disciplined differently than boys for the identical situation.

Time Required:
1½ hours

Number Of Participants:
Minimum of 20

Materials:
1. An equal number of Forms A and B of "Student Case Examples for Problem Solving: Elementary" for a total number equivalent to all participants.
2. One Scoring Key for each.
3. Newsprint or chalkboard, prepared in advance, see Step 4.

Process:

1. The workshop facilitator/trainer explains the first two objectives for the exercise.

2. The facilitator/trainer distributes copies of the "Student Case Examples for Problem Solving" (and answer slips) which have previously been stacked so that Form A alternates with Form B. This insures that an equal number of participants will respond to basically similar case examples with the exception of different gender. Participants are asked to read and follow directions. Allow 15 minutes.

3. Participants are asked to note whether they took Form A or B and form into two (or more) subgroups with participants using same form. Scoring Keys are distributed to each group member. Participants are asked to discuss each response alternatives "goodness" against a criteria of best solution for student growth and eliminating sex-stereotypes. They should be encouraged to agree or disagree with the Scoring Key and state their reasons.

4. The entire group reassembles and by raising hands the following information is tallied on newsprint or chalkboard for the group to analyze. At this time the differences between Forms A and B should be explained.

Example:

Item No.	Student Believed to be (male) — a b c d		Student Believed to be (female) — a b d c	
1	Form A ▯▯▯▯		Form B ▯▯▯▯	
2	Form B ▯▯▯▯		Form A ▯▯▯▯	
3	Form A ▯▯▯▯		Form B ▯▯▯▯	
4	Form B ▯▯▯▯		Form A ▯▯▯▯	
5	Form A ▯▯▯▯		Form B ▯▯▯▯	
6	Form B ▯▯▯▯		Form A ▯▯▯▯	

5. Participants analyze the above information, as follows:

   a. As a group, do we tend to think a male and a female should receive different treatment when sent out of classroom for discipline? Why?

   b. Is a girl who has fears relative to the opposite sex treated the same as a boy?

   c. Is a boy's desire to participate in non-traditional play for his gender treated the same as a girl's? Is it easier for a girl to be labeled "Tomboy" than for a boy to be labeled "sissy?"

   d. Is there a tendency for us to be less willing to encourage males to do housework than to encourage females to work outside the home at non-traditional sex related chores?

   e. Are we more inclined to encourage a male to be affectionate than to encourage a female to be strong enough to defend self? Do we allow one sex or other greater freedom in expressing personality characteristics traditionally sex-stereotyped?

   Note: The response alternatives to case example one do not vary along a continuum of traditional versus non-traditional treatment of gender as do the other five.

6. Encourage participants to share reactions to exercise; then ask each participant to write out in a sentence or two an action plan relative to the insights achieved in the exercise. For example, "I plan to analyze all conduct grades I reported in the last six weeks by sex, or, I plan to record my remarks to students for a day to see if I use praise differently with boys and girls, etc." Allow participants to share these ideas with each other.

STUDENT CASE EXAMPLES FOR PROBLEM SOLVING: ELEMENTARY FORM A

Directions: Six case study situations involving one particular student follow. Four choices follow each item. In some cases you may like several of the choices or none. You must, however, select the one which in your opinion is best.

1. Thomas is sent to the principal's office for spanking by the fourth grade teacher. He explains to the principal, "All the time she asks me to do my work over 'cause she says it's too messy . . . and I do . . . I don't think being neat is so important but I do it over anyway when she tells me to. But today, I just got mad at her. It was my story, see, and she said we could illustrate it any way we wanted to. Then she said mine wasn't pretty and she was sure I could do better if I tried again. I didn't get fresh

155

like she said—well, not at first anyway. I didn't call her stupid until she started calling me names 'cause I said I wouldn't do it over."

What should be done?

a. Paddle the student, but explain first that you are only doing so for calling the teacher names.

b. Advise the student to find better ways to handle frustration and suggest the student apologize. Before the student returns, suggest to the teacher alone that she examine her behavior and suggest alternatives.

c. Inform the student that he was wrong to call the teacher a name and give him a cooling off period before returning to class.

d. Change the student to another fourth grade teacher.

2. Alicia, one of your students, is almost always afraid of something. Sometimes she is afraid of things which it seems likely could never happen. Other times when she seems worried or upset she can't give any reason for it. As her teacher you are concerned enough to request a parent conference. The parents tell you that she is not this way at home, but that often in the morning she says she wants to stay home because the boys are too rough and mean at school.

How do you handle this situation?

a. Involve her in as many mixed sex group activities as possible, but provide extra support and security to allay her anxieties.

b. Do not involve her in the feared activities with boys until she overcomes her fearfulness.

c. Refer her to the school counselor or psychologist for further diagnosis.

d. Do nothing special. She will overcome this with time and calling special attention to this behavior could be harmful.

3. Glen wants to join the girls at jumping rope during recess. The girls refuse to allow him to play and the kids all call him weird.

Which would you be most inclined to do?

a. Invite an amateur or professional boxer to demonstrate his training and workout exercises, including rope jumping.

b. Advise Glen's parents to seek a professional opinion regarding the boy's sex-role confusion.

c. Ask one or two of the more mature boys in the class to encourage Glen to participate in their activities, taking him under their wing and teaching him whatever skills they can.

d. Nothing; allow natural consequences to take their course.

4. Michelle, a fifth grade girl, has a paper route and is the only girl in school

to have one. The other children in the class find out about this and they laugh and tease her.

What do you recommend?

a. A conference with her mother to suggest that she earn money by baby-sitting instead.

b. Assign her chores which allow the others to see her in more traditionally feminine roles, such as passing out milk and housekeeping duties.

c. Praise her before the others, pointing out that her independence will enable her to function well in the world of business. Inform the other children about women role models who did non-traditional things when they were children.

d. Ignore the situation; the other children will soon grow tired of teasing and besides, calling attention to it may cause harm since her family is poor and needs the money.

5. A father drops off his sixth grade son at school every day and kisses the boy good-bye. The other children see and laugh.

How do you handle the situation?

a. Conference with the father and suggest that he not do this before the other children.

b. Speak to the other children and try to encourage them to see expressing affection as part of the masculine sex role.

c. Point out the masculine things the boy does as they occur, like running well, showing leadership, etc., to compensate for their limited awareness.

d. Do nothing; the children will soon grow tired of their teasing.

6. In the first couple of months of school you observe that Patricia, one of your students, likes to show everyone how tough she is. On the playground she always tries to take the lead in games and frequently succeeds in filling the dominant role. Surprisingly, the boys don't seem to mind Patricia's dominance. At least there have been no visible complaints. On a few occasions, Patricia has gotten into fights with others in the class but the causes seem to be related to other things.

What should you do?

a. Don't allow Patricia to play with the boys until her behavior improves.

b. Combine the boys and girls teams. The effects of including other girls should soften Patricia's aggressiveness.

c. Interfere as little as possible. You can rely on the consequences from the girls bringing her into line as the year progresses.

    d. Refer her to the school counselor or psychologist for further diagnosis.

STUDENT CASE EXAMPLES FOR PROBLEM SOLVING: ELEMENTARY FORM B

Directions: Six case study situations involving one particular student follow. Four choices follow each item. In some cases you may like several of the choices or none. You must, however, select the one which in your opinion is best.

1. Cynthia is sent to the principal's office for spanking by the fourth grade grade teacher. She explains to the principal, "All the time she asks me to do my work over 'cause she says it's too messy . . . and I do . . . I don't think being neat is so important but I do it over anyway when she tells me to. But today I just got mad at her. It was my story, see, and she said we could illustrate it any way we wanted to. Then she said mine wasn't pretty and she was sure i could do better if I tried again. I didn't get fresh like she said—well, not at first anyway. I didn't call her stupid until she started calling me names 'cause I said I wouldn't do it over."

    What should be done?

    a. Paddle the student, but explain first that you are only doing so for calling the teacher names.

    b. Advise the student to find better ways to handle frustration and suggest the student apologize. Before the student returns suggest to the teacher alone that she examine her behavior and suggest alternatives.

    c. Inform the student that she was wrong to call the teacher a name and give her a cooling off period before returning to class.

    d. Change the student to another fourth grade teacher.

2. Jorge, one of your students, is almost always afraid of something. Sometimes, he is afraid of things which it seems likely could never happen. Other times when he seems worried or upset he can't give any reason for it. As his teacher you are concerned enough to request a parent conference. The parents tell you that he is not this way at home, but that often in the morning he does not want to go to school because the girls always seem to do everything better than he.

    How do you handle this situation?

    a. Involve him in as many mixed-sex groups as possible but provide support and security to allay anxieties.

    b. Separate him from the feared situations with girls until he acquires more confidence in his abilities.

    c. Refer him to the school counselor or psychologist for further diagnosis.

    d. Do nothing special; he will overcome this with time and calling special attention to this behavior could be harmful.

3. Gwen wants to join the boys at basketball during recess. The boys refuse to allow her to play and the kids all call her weird.

    Which would you do?

    a. Invite an amateur or professional female basketball player to demonstrate techniques for improved playing.

    b. Advise Gwen's parents to seek a professional opinion regarding the girl's sex-role confusion.

    c. Ask one or two of the more mature girls in the class to encourage Gwen to participate in their activities, taking her under their wing and including her whenever they can.

    d. Nothing, natural consequences provide the best learning experience in cases of this sort.

4. Joe, a fifth grade boy, helps his mother to do all the household chores: dusting, vacuuming, washing dishes, cooking, mending, and sorting the laundry. The other children in the class find out about this and they laugh and tease him.

    What do you recommend?

    a. A conference with his mother to ask her to give him different chores.

    b. Assign him chores which allow the others to see him in more traditionally masculine roles such as the heaviest tasks and leadership roles.

    c. Praise him and point out to the other children that Joe will be more independent as a bachelor. Encourage them to share with each other the fact that they probably all do household chores; also, call attention to male models who fill non-traditional roles at home.

    d. Ignore the situation; the children will cease their behavior and calling attention may only cause harm since Joe's mother works and he has no father.

5. A girl in the sixth grade changes in the girl's bathroom in preparation for her Karate class to which her mother takes her directly after picking her up. The other children see and laugh.

    How do you handle the situation?

a. Conference with the mother and suggest that the girl change her lesson time so the children will not know.

b. Speak to the class and encourage them to broaden their perception of sex-roles to include a girl taking Karate.

c. Point out the more feminine things which she does as they occur in the classroom, even her appearance and dress.

d. Do nothing; the children will soon grow tired of their teasing.

6. In the first couple of months of school you observe that one of your students, Patrick, likes to show everyone how tough he is on the playground. He always tries to take the lead in games and frequently succeeds. Surprisingly, the boys don't seem to mind Patrick's dominance. At least, they haven't visibly complained yet. On a few occasions Patrick has gotten into fights with the other students but the causes seem to be related to other things.

What should you do?

a. Encourage similar leadership in the other boys as related to games and playground activities while channeling their aggression.

b. Combine boys and girls teams into one. The effects on including girls should decrease Patrick's aggressiveness.

c. Refer him to school counselor or psychologist for further diagnosis.

d. Interfere as little as possible; you can rely on the consequences from his fellow students to bring him into line as the year progresses.

SCORING KEY — Elementary:

Item No.*	Response Alternative			
	a	b	c	d
1 (male)	0	2	2	2
(female)	4	1	1	2
2	3	0	2	1
3	4	0	1	1
4	0	1	4	1
5	0	3	1	1
6 (male)	1	3	2	2
(female)	0	3	1	0

0 = Practice *very* much reinforces traditional sex-role stereotypes

1 = Practice *somewhat* reinforces traditional sex-role stereotypes

2 = Practice is *neutral* as regards sex-role stereotyping

3 = Practice encourages *some* departure from traditional sex-role stereotypes

4 = Practice *very much* encourages departure from traditional sex-role stereotypes

*Scoring for items 1 and 6 differs depending if the item is male or female. Scoring on items 2, 3, 4, 5 does not differ depending if the item is male or female.

28

How Do I Like Thee? Examining And Understanding Preferences

Objectives For Educators:

1. To analyze character qualities and traits of preferred students by gender.
2. To compare above patterns by sex with clinicians' descriptions of the healthy adult, the healthy adult male, and the healthy adult female.
3. To acquire insights and understanding regarding the emotional patterns of their students.

Time Required:

2 hours

Number Of Participants:

Minimum of 15

Materials:

1. For each participant: 8 slips of paper, pencils, and the "Adjective Check-list."
2. Three previously headed newsprint sheets for each sub-group; see steps 3, 6, and 12.

Process:
1. The workshop facilitator introduces the activity by explaining its purposes. This explanation should include the following: "While few of us like to admit to student preferences, we all have them. By examining our preferences we are usually able to govern our behavior more wisely."
2. Eight slips of paper are distributed to each participant. Participants are told that only they will see their own writing but that the information learned minus student names will be used by the group. Participants are then asked to write the names of their two most preferred students on separate slips of paper and the names of their two least preferred students on two slips of paper. After this is completed, teachers are instructed to write the first three characteristics about each of these students that come to mind. Allow only two minutes and be sure to emphasize spontaneous writing of the characteristics.
3. On newsprint the facilitator will tally the number of most and least preferred students by sex. Participants are asked to raise their hands for the count.

   Example:

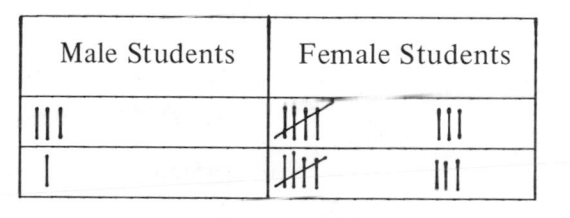

	Male Students	Female Students
Most preferred	III	JHT III
Least preferred	I	JHT III

4. The teacher/participants are asked to look at their four slips already written and write the names of four more students so that a balance of the following is achieved:

   two most preferred female students
   two least preferred female students

   two most preferred male students
   two least preferred male students

5. Once again participants are asked to write the first three characteristics which come to mind which describe these four students whose names they have just written.
6. Participants are now asked to form subgroups of from ten to fifteen members. Each subgroup chooses a recorder who writes the student characteristics in the appropriate box on the group's newsprint summary sheet. The heavily tallied trait descriptions in each box should be circled.

	Male Students	Female Students
Most Preferable Characteristics	enthusiastic hard-working creative funny	sensitive to others gentle hard-working helpful
Least Preferable Characteristics	sullen critical	bossy phony

7. After the subgroups have had a chance to discuss their results, noting patterns, etc., the workshop facilitator interrupts to present the following information to the entire group:

Read: Seventy clinical psychologists were polled for their judgement of what characteristics were most representative of healthy adult males and healthy adult females. After that they were asked to define the healthy adult.* In this study, designed by Inge and Broverman at Worcester State Hospital, they found that these patterns emerged from the 122 items the clinical psychologists were given to use in their descriptions:

Show on Newsprint:

1. Non-aggressive
2. Unable to separate feelings from ideas
3. Strong need for security
4. Tactful and gentle
5. Dependent
6. Manipulative
7. Spiritual

1. Aggressive
2. Non-emotional and objective
3. Has little need for security
4. Independent
5. Competitive
6. Logical
7. Self-confident

Read: The Broverman study also found that the clinicians' concepts of a healthy adult male were not significantly different from their concept of a healthy adult. But their concepts of a healthy adult woman were definitely different from what they felt made a healthy adult.

---

* I. K. Broverman et al. "Sex-role Stereotypes and Clinical Judgements of Mental Health," *Journal of Consulting and Clinical Psychology*, American Psychological Association, 1970, *34*, 1-7.

8. The workshop facilitator asks each group to display for the entire group their results and a brief discussion comparing workshop findings with the Broverman study follows.

9. The workshop facilitator now tells participants that at least part of our reluctance to reveal "less preference" for some students stems from our positive belief as educators that it is our job to understand students. And, in fact, when we think about it, understanding students better usually reduces the intensity of low preference feelings.

   Teacher participants are now asked to take the same slips on which they wrote the names and three descriptive words about the eight students and turn over the most and least preferred of each sex (total = 4). On the backs they are asked to choose, from the Adjective Checklist which they will now receive, the emotions which are most characteristic of these same students. For some students they may write many; for others they may need only a few. (They will overlap if emotion-words were used on the other side.) Tell them to ignore the letter symbols before each adjective for now.

10. When step nine is completed, give the following information to teachers and ask them to think briefly about each student's emotional pattern and find if they come to any new insights about the student.

    Information to read and post:

    Emotional Patterns By Symbol*

    (A) = active-happy
    (D) = sad-depressed
    (H) = angry-hostile
    (F) = fatigued
    (T) = anxious-tense

11. Teacher-participants are asked to reform into their subgroups and this time share their insights and suggestions for meeting student's emotional needs.

12. Following the discussion each subgroup again chooses a recorder who writes the emotion patterns in the appropriate boxes of a new newsprint summary sheet.

---

*Adapted from L. A. Gottshalk, and G. C. Gleser, *The Measurement of Psychological States Through the Content Analysis of Verbal Behavior* (Berkeley and Los Angeles: University of California Press, 1969), p. 148.

Example:

	Males	Females
Emotional patterns of most preferred		
Emotional patterns of least preferred		

13. The workshop facilitator asks each subgroup to post and share their group's results with the entire group. Participants now share reactions to this second half of the exercise on understanding students' emotions; relating it to sex of students; and most and least preferred categories.

Adjective Checklist*

(A) 1. active
(A) 2. adventurous
(T) 3. afraid
(A) 4. alert
(A) 5. ambitious
(H) 6. angry
(H) 7. annoyed
(T) 8. anxious
(H) 9. bitter
(D) 10. blue
(-T) 11. calm
(A) 12. cheerful
(A) 13. confident
(A) 14. contented
(D) 15. dejected
(D) 16. despondent
(D) 17. discouraged
(H) 18. disgusted
(F) 19. dull
(A) 20. energetic
(A) 21. enthusiastic
(T) 22. fretful
(-H) 23. friendly
(T) 24. frightened

(H) 25. furious
(D) 26. gloomy
(H) 27. grouchy
(A) 28. happy
(T) 29. helpless
(D) 30. hopeless
(H) 31. impatient
(H) 32. irritable
(A) 33. joyous
(A) 34. lighthearted
(A) 35. lively
(D) 36. lonely
(H) 37. mean
(A) 38. merry
(D) 39. miserable
(D) 40. moody
(T) 41. nervous
(T) 42. on edge
(T) 43. panicky
(A) 44. peaceable
(-H) 45. pleasant
(F) 46. plodding
(H) 47. quarrelsome
(H) 48. rebellious

(-T) 49. relaxed
(H) 50. resentful
(T) 51. restless
(D) 52. sad
(-T) 53. secure
(T) 54. shaky
(F) 55. sleepy
(F) 56. slow
(F) 57. sluggish
(D) 58. sorrowful
(T) 59. tense
(T) 60. threatened
(F) 61. tired
(-H) 62. tolerant
(T) 63. uneasy
(D) 64. unhappy
(A) 65. up
(T) 66. upset
(D) 67. useless
(F) 68. weary
(T) 69. worried
(D) 70. worthless

*Ibid.

How Do I Read Thee? Understanding Student Behavior

Objectives For Educators:

1. To identify expectancies for the following self-defeating behaviors to be related to gender and analyze validity and/or rationale of such expectancies: hostility directed outward, hostility towards self, anxiety.
2. To assess his/her individual ability to recognize the presence of the above emotions in students' verbalizations.
3. To relate one's ability to recognize emotion with one's current emotional state.

Time Required:

1½ hours

Number Of Participants:

Minimum of 20

Materials:

1. Assessment tool—"Identification of Emotions in Student Verbal Content"
2. "Scoring Key"
3. "Emotional Definitions"
4. "Adjective Checklist" (Exercise 28)
5. Newsprint and magic markers

Process:

    1. The workshop facilitator will introduce the objectives of the activity. The facilitator explains further that one important function of the educator is is to identify students with special needs, and that one purpose of this exercise is to focus on the early recognition of students who: (a) might suffer from excessive anxiety which may interfere with cognitive functioning; (b) have hostile feelings which they tend to direct towards the outside world and (c) have hostile feelings which they tend to direct towards themselves—a prelude generally to depression.

    2. The facilitator/trainer distributes copies of the "Identification of Emotion from Students' Verbal Content," which have been previously stacked so that form A alternates with form B. This insures that an equal number of participants will respond to identical student excerpts labeled male on one form and female on the other. The participants are asked to read and follow directions. Allow no more than fifteen minutes.

    3. Participants are informed about the construction of and reasons for forms A and B. They are divided into two subgroups by form letter for their group's data analyses on newsprint, as follows:

Sample

Item No.	Tally						Group Total pts.	Average = Group Total ÷ No. in Group
	0	1	2	3	4	5		
1.Anxiety Hostility Inward Hostility Outward 2.	|	|||				|		16	16 ·/. 10= 1 3/5

    4. The entire group reassembles and combines subgroup data as follows:

Item No.	Average	Average
1. Anxiety	1.5	3.5
Hostility outward	2.0	1.0
Hostility inward	2.5	3.5

At this same time each participant is given a copy of the "Scoring Key" and the "Emotional Definitions."

5. A discussion among the participants follows the above comparison.

- Further clarification and definition of hostility and anxiety
- How is each harmful?
- What can or should educators do when they identify a student with excessive anxiety, etc.?
- What results from expecting one sex or the other to exhibit more of one of these emotions?
- What relationship does the educator's emotional state have to their ability to identify emotion?

6. As a follow-up to the last point in number 5, above: each participant is given a copy of "Adjective Checklist," and asked to circle those emotions which he/she feels are most characteristic of his/her present emotional state. Participants are asked to ignore the letter symbols before each word for now.

7. The facilitator/trainer reports the meaning of the letter symbols, as follows: (A) = active-happy; (D) = sad-depressed; (H) = angry-hostile; (F) = fatigued; (T) = anxious-tense; and encourages each person to briefly analyze their emotional pattern and decide for themselves whether it may have influenced their ability to recognize the emotions of students in the exercise.

8. Participants are invited to share comments and reactions to the activity.

Note: Participants should be cautioned not to overgeneralize from one bit of information.

IDENTIFYING EMOTIONS IN STUDENT VERBAL CONTENT

Note: Enough space is left before each excerpt below for the purpose of constructing two forms by adding the identification as follows:

Form A	Form B
1. Cleveland, a fifth grade boy	1. Cynthia, a fifth grade girl
2. Henry, a male student in eighth grade	2. Helen, a female student in eighth grade
3. Jorge, a seventh grade male	3. Alicia, a seventh grade female
4. Jill, a female in eighth grade	4. John, a male in eighth grade
5. Michael, a boy in fifth grade	5. Michelle, a girl in fifth grade
6. Virginia, a sixth grade girl	6. Virgil, a sixth grade boy

Directions:

The following excerpts are students' 5-minute responses to open-ended directions to tell something about themselves. The teacher may have asked students to take turns sharing in small, get-acquainted groups or assigned an autobiographical topic for written expression, such as: "Tell the most important thing that happened in the last year," or "What did you do on your summer vacation?"

Read each of the student responses below and circle the number in the right-hand column which you feel best represents degree of the emotions specified.

1. This will be a story about how I feel in this new school. Well, I try to do good in school but I don't seem to know how to do it. It seems like everything I say or do might be wrong. Then I'd be wrong, see, cause that's all I've ever done is wrong things mostly. And I guess that's why I got punished so much before. I don't know what's the matter with me. I was hoping I wouldn't be messing up like this here. I don't mean to skip so much. That time I stole the clothes I wouldn't have done nothing like that if I hadn't been skipping school. It was just too much of everything and I didn't know what to do. My nerves were getting bad like they do when I think I'm gonna flunk. As much wrong as I've been doing, I guess I'll just have to take what the principal gives me. Maybe I'd do better if my Mom hadn't left. If she'd stayed with us I bet I'd been a good student like the other kids. I just never made it that's all.

	NONE	LOW	MEDIUM	HIGH

Anxiety:
0 1 2 3 4 5

Hostility to Others/ Things:
0 1 2 3 4 5

Hostility Towards Self:
0 1 2 3 4 5

2. During the summer, my grandmother was very sick in the hospital and I was supposed to go see her. But before my parents ever got a chance to take me there she died. So I didn't get to see her before she died. I went to the funeral but we didn't see her then either because they had the casket shut. And then, let's see another time one evening some friends and I went to the youth club. And there was this girl there that we knew dancing the bump with this guy. It wasn't very nice. And all these other guys kept egging her on. And then one time at the youth club the police arrested two people, a girl and a boy. Now the youth club is being investigated because the police say that some of the kids there are smoking pot. They might get closed down. My mother says it's a terrible place and she doesn't want me to go there anymore. It used to be a pretty nice place for kids to go after school.

	NONE	LOW	MEDIUM	HIGH

Anxiety:

0 1 2 3 4 5

Hostility to Others/ Things:

0 1 2 3 4 5

Hostility Towards Self:

0 1 2 3 4 5

3. It's my turn? Well, okay—but if I
knew something to talk about, I
could tell it better. I don't know
whether all of you are interested or
not, and I feel stupid sitting here like
this. Everything I know about myself
I like to keep to myself. But I guess
you're trying to find out something
about me. Well, I went to music camp
this last summer but the piano teacher
was really disgusted with my playing,
cause I didn't practice enough like I
should have. I guess it sounds like I
don't behave but of what little I did
this summer, camp was the highlight.
Oh, I played baseball. As a matter of
fact I got hit in the head with a baseball. Then I got sunburned [laughs].
I mean I was a technicolor mess part
of the summer . . . black and blue
marks all over red. I guess you'll
think I'm a real complainer, but that's
the honest truth of what happened on
the first summer I was sent off to
sleep away camp.

	NONE	LOW	MEDIUM	HIGH
Anxiety:	0	1 2	3	4 5
Hostility to Others/ Things:	0	1 2	3	4 5
Hostility Towards Self:	0	1 2	3	4 5

4. This is going to be a story about when I was in the children's home. That's before I got put in the foster group home where I am now. Once we were doing something on bicycles and the manager grabbed us and started to whip us. And then I argued with him him so he made us all stay in bed all day. And then another time we was out in the park and I was shooting off arrows at another kid. I hit him in the cheek so I got whipped again. After that I just ran away. Me and a friend stole a moped, but I got mad at Terry and we split up. But the cops got both of us anyway and brought us back. Terry got sent to state school then. I ran over a cat while I was driving and I didn't feel so good about that. Then the tire got a flat and that's when they caught me. I'm glad I didn't get sent to the state school, cause I'm pretty sure I wouldn't like it at all. Every day is just alike, the same things unless you get into fights or something. They have a system of swats, if you do something wrong or else they take away your privileges.

				M		
				E		
	N			D	H	
	O	L		I	I	
	N	O		U	G	
	E	W		M	H	

Anxiety: _____
0 1 2 3 4 5

Hostility to Others/ Things: _____
0 1 2 3 4 5

Hostility Towards Self: _____
0 1 2 3 4 5

5. I'll tell the story of my life, okay?
When I was a young girl—before
kindergarten—my mom and dad
were really poor. We lived in two
rooms and it wasn't nice and we
had a hard time of it. I got picked
on a lot by the other kids there.
That's why I am like I am. I mean
I'm not bad or anything like that,
but I worry a lot that I'm not gonna
do good enough. At night I lay in
bed and think about all the things I
should do the next day; homework I
must do and things like that. I can't
stand to get bawled out. That's my
worst fault. When somebody yells at
me or bawls me out, I just can't
stand it. I make mistakes I know,
but I've never had a time when I just
had good times. I've always had to
do without and make things do. But
I've tried as hard and as best as I
possibly could.

	NONE	LOW	MEDIUM	HIGH
Anxiety:	0	1 2	3 4	5
Hostility to Others/ Things:	0	1 2	3 4	5
Hostility Towards Self:	0	1 2	3 4	5

6. Well, let's see. I went traveling in an
airplane 2,000 miles and that gave me
an interesting experience with people.
A pretty frightening experience was
when one of the plane engines was
found not working right and we
learned just over the mountains that
it had only been fixed temporarily.
Some of the passengers were really
frightened but others acted as if they
didn't have a worry in the world.
However, that was only a little bit of
my summer even though interesting.
Let's see, I have to think what else to
tell you. A rather interesting thing
too was that a group of us went to
the pool every week to swim and
practice diving. Pat, my friend, always got the worst of it. Diving and
Pat just didn't go together. Pat was
always bruised and limping after-
wards. Another time we were playing tennis. Pat went down skinning
both arms badly. We did some real
kidding about it. Grace, you know?

	NONE	LOW	MEDIUM	HIGH
Anxiety:	0	1 2	3 4	5

Hostility to Others/ Things:

0 1 2 3 4 5

Hostility Towards Self:

0 1 2 3 4 5

SCORING KEY*

Numbers are not used below because they imply a precision beyond what is needed by the teacher.

1.	Anxiety	— Medium/high	4.	Anxiety	— Low
	Hostility outward	— None		Hostility outward	— High
	Hostility to self	— High		Hostility to self	— None
2.	Anxiety	— Medium/low	5.	Anxiety	— Medium/low
	**Hostility outward	— Medium/low		Hostility outward	— None
	Hostility to self	— None		Hostility to self	— Medium/high
3.	Anxiety	— High	6.	Anxiety	— Medium
	Hostility outward	— Low		Hostility outward	— None
	Hostility to self	— Medium		Hostility to self	— None

    *The standards for the student excerpts on anxiety, hostility directed outward, and hostility directed inward were taken from verbal samples coded for anxiety, hostility directed outward, and hostility directed inward, respectively, in the *Manual of Instructions for Using the Gottschalk-Gleser Content Analysis Scales: Anxiety, Hostility, and Social Alienation/Personal Disorganization*, by Louis A. Gottschalk, Carolyn N. Winget and Goldine C. Gleser, University of California Press, Berkeley and Los Angeles, 1969. They were adapted to appear as student verbal samples for the purpose of this exercise.

    **This particular response is interesting because all hostility is indirect. A pattern of expressing hostility more typically female. In this case the girl refers to being disappointed by others and others "misbehaving" and being punished.

Emotions Defined*

Anxiety. No attempt made to differentiate between fear and anxiety. Six verbal subcategories defined are:

(1) *Separation anxiety*—references to desertion, abandonment, loneliness, ostracism, loss of support, falling, loss of love or love object, or threat of such.

(2) *Guilt anxiety*—references to adverse criticism, condemnation, moral disapproval, guilt, or threat of such.

(3) *Shame anxiety*—references to ridicule, inadequacy, shame, embarrassment, humiliation, over-exposure of deficiencies or private details.

(4) *Diffuse anxiety*—references by word or phrases to anxiety and/or fear without distinguishing type or source.

(5) *Death anxiety*—references to death, dying, threat of death or anxiety about it.

(6) *Mutilation anxiety*—references to injury, tissue or physical damage, or anxiety about injury or threat of same.

It is assumed that there is more intense anxiety when the person reports being directly threatened and that anxiety is less when the person refers to it indirectly; for example, speaking in terms of others being hurt or objects injured. Even the denial of anxiety is assumed to indicate a low level or otherwise it would not be mentioned at all.

Keep in mind that a single situation is not a good indicator of a subject's typical level of anxiety. This would require a number of occasions over an extended period of time.

Hostility—Outward. Verbal hostility directed outward ranges on a continuum that varies from strong expressions of physical and verbal aggression towards human beings through expressions of mild dislike or criticism of an individual, through hostility toward a situation or infrahuman objects, through references to anger without an object, and finally to denial of hostility. Statements that refer to the aggressive or hostile feelings as having emanated from the speaker are classified as overt hostility directed outward, while aggression or hostility attributed to others as either active agents or passive recipients and the denial of hostility are classified as covert hostility.

---

*Definitions adapted from the respective scales used to classify verbal content of 5-minute duration. L. A. Gottschalk, C. N. Winget, and G. C. Gleser, *The Manual of Instructions for Using the Gottschalk-Gleser Content Analysis Scales: Anxiety, Hostility and Social Alienation—Personal Disorganization* (Berkeley and Los Angeles, Calif.: University of California Press, 1969).

Hostility—Inward. Verbal hostility directed inward refers to transient and immediate thoughts, actions and feelings that are self-critical, self-destructive or self-punishing. It has been found to relate strongly to depression and is often considered the precursor to depression. It has also been used synonomously with the term "masochism." Hostility directed inward ranges in intensity from statements about being painfully driven or obliged to meet one's standards or expectations, denials of hostility toward self or feelings of disappointment; through stronger feelings of deprivation, disappointment, lonesomeness, self-criticism, to a great degree of depression or more intense self-criticisms and/or references to self-injury. The strongest form is, of course, references to self-elimination.

30

Are You In The Process Of Rearing A Male Chauvinist?

Objectives For Parents:

1. To acquire increased understanding of the primary role they play in the career aspirations and eventual career decisions of their sons.
2. To identify their tendencies to teach and reinforce traditionally sex-stereotyped occupations.
3. To be provided with a means of identifying tendencies to stereotype occupations in their sons.
4. To explore implications of the acquisition of occupationally sex-stereotyped attitudes that the male should dominate the world of work.

Objectives For Educators:

1. To communicate objectives of teaching for sex-role expansion to parents.
2. To involve parents in recognizing the important role they play in their child's education.

Time Required:
1½ hours

Number Of Participants:
Unlimited

Materials:

One copy for each participant of the following:

1. "I'd Like My Son to Think About A _____ Career"
2. "Scoring Instructions," to accompany above
3. "When I Grow Up I'd Like To Be _____ (for males)" with directions attached.
4. Discussion topics on slips of paper (or newsprint) for distribution to groups; see step 7.

Process:

1. The educator will want to inform parents in a 5-minute lecturette that they, more than any other factor, influence the ways in which their children learn adult sex-roles and make career choices. Research tends to support the common sense assumption that parents and the role models and guidance they offer children have the most significant impact.

   The following points can be brought out:

   - A democratic parent-son relationship is more conducive to achievement behaviors than is an autocratic relationship.*

   - Research has not identified any one overriding influence but by asking individuals what factors most influenced their choice of vocation in a research study, Borow isolated four factors.** These are: outside work experience; school studies and factors related to school; parents; and other significant persons. Paramount among these were the family factors, although their influence wanes after early adolescence.

   - By providing certain types of play materials and experiences parents may orient their child's interest from the early years. For example, camping in the wilds may encourage an interest in forestry or one of the natural science occupations; large home libraries—in use—may spark a desire towards an academic profession; and a chemistry set can start a child dreaming. A survey of outstanding achievers in a wide variety of fields revealed that all reported a significant adult— usually a parent—who was intensely involved in the area of their achievement and who shared this involvement with them as a child.

---

*R. A. Rehberg, J. Sinclair, and W. E. Shafer, "Adolescent Achievement Behavior, Family Authority Structure and Parental Socialization Practices," *American Journal of Sociology*, 1970, 75(6), 1012-1034.

**H. Borow (Ed.), *Man in a World at Work* (Boston: Houghton Mifflin, 1964).

2. After communicating the importance of parental influence especially in the early years, the educator will explain the exercise objectives and format; adding that while many people say they don't care what occupation their children pursue as long as they're happy, they rarely are without some preferences. And to remain unconscious about our preferences is not to be able to exercise control over them.

3. Copies of "I'd Like My Son to Think About A _____ Career," are distributed to each parent. (Parents without sons are asked to either think of themselves, a male child to whom they're close, their daughter's future husband, or the son they would like to have.)

4. Parents are instructed not to unstaple the strip of paper folded over the last column. Each parent is told to read each item and circle or check the face which most nearly approximates their feeling of whether they would like, not like, or be indifferent to their son's considering that occupational area. Allow three minutes for everyone to finish.

5. Parents are now instructed to open the stapled over column and to indicate by circle or check whether they think this occupation is best performed by a man, a woman, or either one. Remind them that they alone will see their score and that they should go with their first and true feeling. Allow two minutes for everyone to finish.

6. A scoring sheet is distributed to each parent. The educator will go through the scoring procedure with parents step by step. Allow 10 to 15 minutes.

7. Parents are asked to form groups of ten or twelve and each group is given one of the following topics for discussion. Each group is asked to choose a leader to facilitate discussion and report the group's conclusions to the entire group. Allow at least 20 minutes.

   a. Parents who put too heavy an emphasis on the male as dominant in the world of work usually pass this attitude on to their sons. The result for the son is that he will also put too heavy an emphasis on career— becoming a workaholic to the exclusion of other activities in his life style. Do you think this is true or not? If so, what can be done about it?

   b. Parents who put too heavy an emphasis on the male as dominant in the world of work usually pass this attitude along to their sons. The result is that sons feel like a failure if they are not able to be the sole provider or if their wives have equal or better socioeconomic status in the world of work. Do you think this is true or not? If so, what can be done about it?

   c. Parents who put too heavy an emphasis on the male as dominant in the world of work usually pass this attitude on to their daughters. Their daughters in turn look for and expect the male to be provider and protector and are more likely to be intolerant of males and husbands who fall short of their ideal. Do you think this is true? If so, what can or should be done about it?

    d. A too heavy emphasis on the male as dominant in the world of work in parental attitudes lead to pressure on sons to consider salary and status as primary factors in career choice. The result is that many males have unrealistic career aspirations which doom them to feelings of inadequacy. Do you think this is true? If so, what can or should be done about it?

    e. Parents who put too heavy an emphasis on the male as dominant in the world of work usually pass this attitude on to their sons. One result is that sons are limited in terms of their selection of a mate with whom they will be compatible. Do you think this is true? If so, what can or should be done about it?

    f. Parents who put too heavy an emphasis on the male as dominant in the world of work usually pass this attitude along to their sons. The result is that the sons will exclude themselves from many areas of homemaking and family life which are clearly preferable to some of the work options open to males.

8. The spokesman for each group reports to the entire group. This is followed by a discussion of and reaction to the findings by the entire group. The educator will want to point out that research findings indicate a trend in the direction stated in each of the discussion topics.

9. Each parent is now give a copy of "When I Grow Up, I'd Like To Be _____ (for males)." They are told that directions for administration are attached and that the scoring is the same as theirs. Parents are encouraged to administer it to their son and compare similarities and differences of their own score to that of their sons.

SCORING INSTRUCTIONS

I. *Who Needs Bifocals?* Score 1 point each if you circled items 1, 2, 6, and 10 as best done by females and items 3, 4, 5, 7, 8, and 9 as best done by males. This score indicates the extent to which you see jobs in traditional sex-role stereotypes.

II. *All Power to the Men.* Score 1 point each for items 4, 5, and 7 if circled as most appropriate jobs for males. This score indicates the extent to which you see mind, body, and soul affairs (high-level decision-making jobs for others) as best conducted by males.

III. *Gird Up Your Loins, Boys (or the Good Old Boys' Club).* Score 1 point each for items 3, 4, 5, 7, 8, and 9 if they reflect a "gird up your loins, boys" pattern; that is, I would not like the job at all but it's men's work . . .

Gird Up Your Loins   

OR — I would like it very much and it's a job that belongs to us men.

Good Old Boys Club

IV. *Thank Heaven for Little Girls (or I'm No Sissy).* Score 1 point each if items 1, 2, 6, and 10 show you "saved" from "women's work"; that is, I would like to do it but it's women's work . . .

I'm No Sissy

OR — I wouldn't like it and men don't have to do it.

Thank Heaven For Little Girls

Total the above scores and compare them to the following scale:

8 or below — surprisingly free from stereotypes; some woman is sure to send flowers.

8 through 12 — you reflect the traditional chauvinism of our culture.

13 through 17 — check tail bone for a beginning curly tail.

Directions:

Take a few minutes before beginning, to be sure that your child understands the concept of job or occupation as including the work a person does on a regular basis to earn money and/or to give meaning to their lives. Give two or three illustrations that are not jobs in the quiz and check her understanding by asking her to name some jobs.

With the last column folded back, *say*: "Look at this first job. It is a child care worker." Then *read* the job description aloud to your child. *Say*: "When you grow up, do you think you would like this job very much? If so, put a mark on this face. If you think you would not like this job at all, put a mark on this face. If you're not sure or feel in between, put a mark on this face. YOU MIGHT LIKE ALL OF THEM, NONE OF THEM, OR JUST NOT BE SURE. WHATEVER YOU THINK OR FEEL IS OKAY." Have your child go on and do the other nine the same way.

Now unfold the last column and *say*: "Look at each job again [read each job description as you do the items one by one] and circle whether you think this job could be done *best* by a man, a woman or either one."

I'd Like My Son To Think About A _____ Career.

1		Child care specialist: nursery school, infant care		
2		Food service worker: food server, bar personnel, cook, maitre d'		
3		Sanitation worker		
4		Minister, priest, rabbi		
5		Business executive, administrator or one with managerial responsibility		

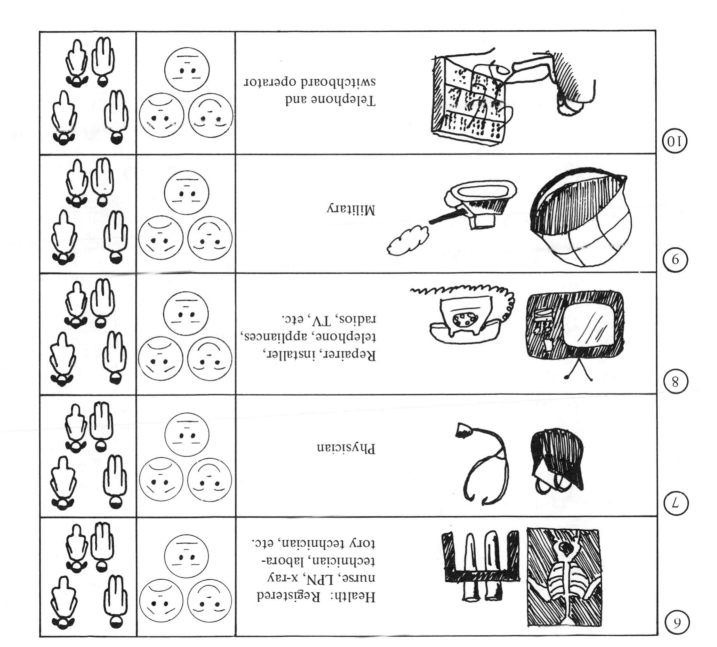

When I Grow Up I'd Like To Be _____ (for males)

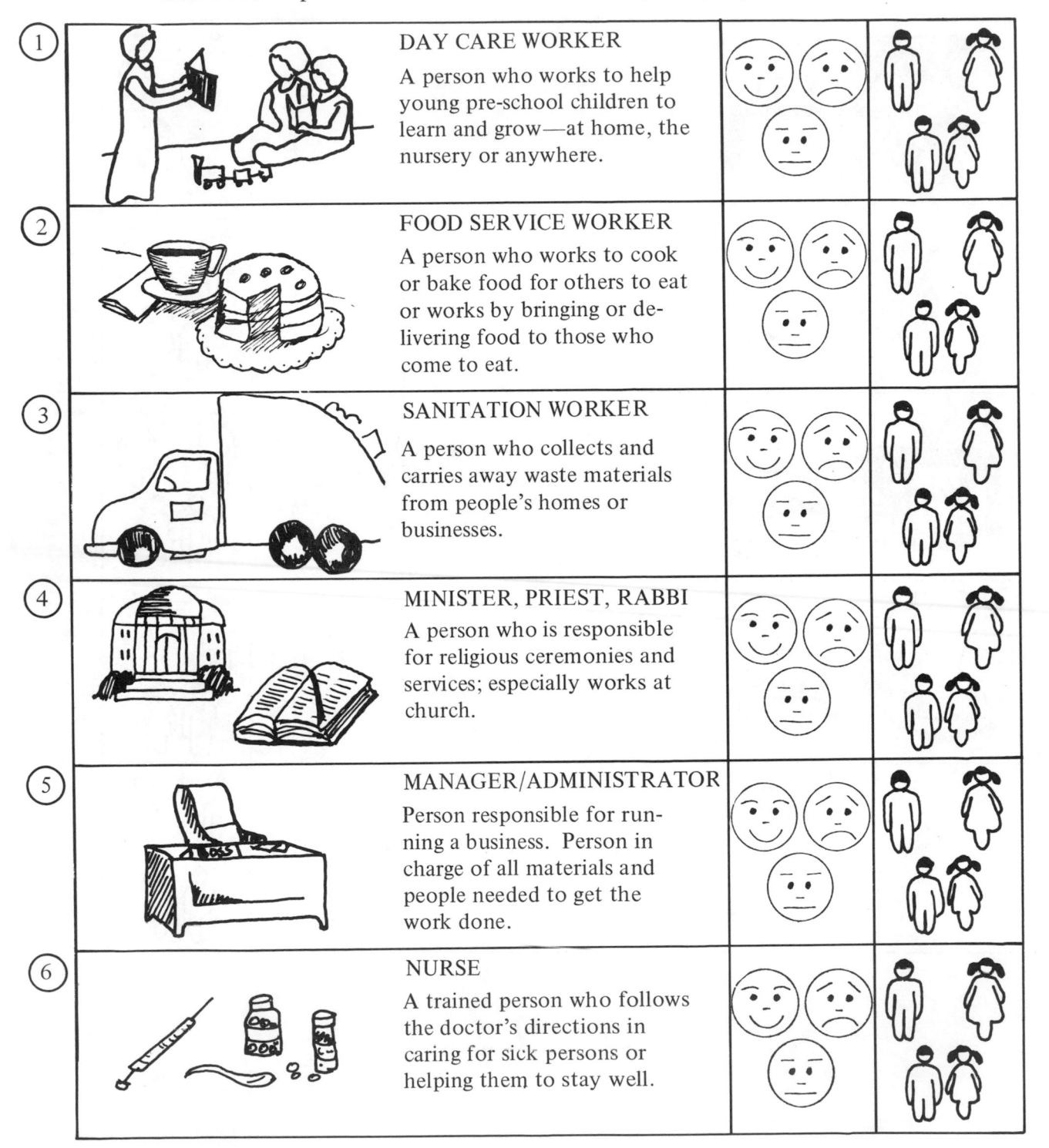

1. **DAY CARE WORKER**
A person who works to help young pre-school children to learn and grow—at home, the nursery or anywhere.

2. **FOOD SERVICE WORKER**
A person who works to cook or bake food for others to eat or works by bringing or delivering food to those who come to eat.

3. **SANITATION WORKER**
A person who collects and carries away waste materials from people's homes or businesses.

4. **MINISTER, PRIEST, RABBI**
A person who is responsible for religious ceremonies and services; especially works at church.

5. **MANAGER/ADMINISTRATOR**
Person responsible for running a business. Person in charge of all materials and people needed to get the work done.

6. **NURSE**
A trained person who follows the doctor's directions in caring for sick persons or helping them to stay well.

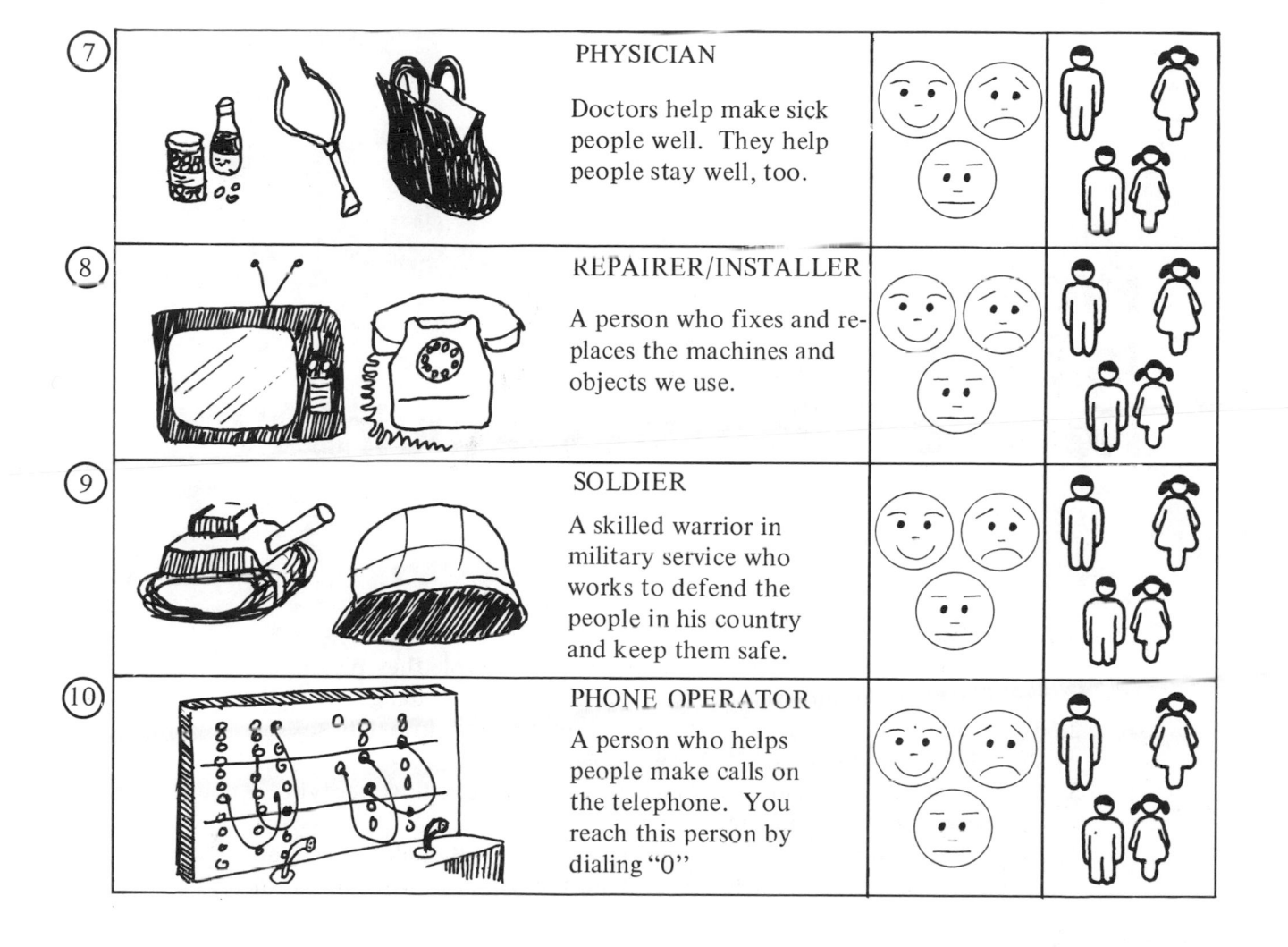

(7) **PHYSICIAN**

Doctors help make sick people well. They help people stay well, too.

(8) **REPAIRER/INSTALLER**

A person who fixes and replaces the machines and objects we use.

(9) **SOLDIER**

A skilled warrior in military service who works to defend the people in his country and keep them safe.

(10) **PHONE OPERATOR**

A person who helps people make calls on the telephone. You reach this person by dialing "0"

31

Are You In The Process Of Rearing A Female Chauvinist?

Objectives For Parents:

1. To acquire increased understanding of the primary role they play in the career aspirations and eventual career decisions of their daughters.
2. To identify their tendencies to teach and reinforce traditionally sex-stereotyped occupations.
3. To be provided with a means of identifying tendencies to stereotype occupations in their daughters.
4. To explore implications of the acquisition of occupationally sex-stereotyped attitudes that a female's most important career is wife and mother.

Objectives For Educators:

1. To communicate objectives of teaching for sex-role expansion.
2. To involve parents in recognizing the important role they play in their child's education.

Time Required:
90 minutes

Number Of Participants:
Unlimited

Materials:
One copy for each participant of the following:
1. "I'd Like My Daughter to Think About A _____ Career"
2. "Scoring Instructions" to accompany above
3. "When I Grow Up I'd Like To Be _____ (for females)," with directions.
4. "Future Facts for Females"
5. Discussion topics on slips of paper or newsprint for distribution to groups, see step 7.

Process:
Note: The first two steps of this exercise are identical to those of the preceding exercise. See p. 180

3. Copies of "I'd Like My Daughter to Think About A _____ Career" are distributed to each parent. (Parents without daughters are asked to either think of themselves, a female child to whom they are close, their son's future wife, or the daughter they would like to have.)
4. Parents are now instructed to not unstaple the strip of paper folded over the last column. Each parent is told to read each item and circle or check the face which most nearly approximates their feeling of whether they would like, not like, or be indifferent to their daughter's considering that occupational area. Allow three minutes for everyone to finish.
5. Parents are now instructed to open the stapled over column and to indicate by circle or check whether they think this occupation is best performed by a man, a woman, or either one. Remind them that they alone will see their score and that they should go with their first and true feeling. Allow two minutes for everyone to finish.
6. The scoring sheet to accompany the above is distributed to each parent. The educator will go through the scoring procedure with parents step by step. Allow 10 to 15 minutes.
7. Parents are asked to form groups of ten or twelve and each group is given one of the following topics for discussion. Each group is asked to choose a leader to facilitate the discussion and report the group's conclusions to the entire group. Allow at least twenty minutes.

   a. Parents who believe a woman's main career is marriage and child rearing and that involvement in the world of work outside the home is secondary will pass these attitudes on to their daughters. One result will be that their daughters will be more likely to have feelings of inadequacy if their husbands and/or children do not achieve success. Do you believe this is true? If so, what can or should be done about it?
   b. Parents who believe a woman's main career is marriage and child rear-

189

ing and that involvement in the world of work outside the home is secondary will pass these attitudes on to their daughters. One result will be that their daughters will be better able to balance a career and family without internal conflict, guilt feelings and frustration. Do you believe this is true? If so, what can or should be done about it?

c. Parents who believe a woman's main career is marriage and child rearing and that involvement in the world of work outside the home is secondary will pass these attitudes on to their daughters. One result will be that their daughters will receive little orientation to selecting a career until late adolescence and by then they will have excluded themselves from the top level professions or high paying blue collar skill jobs. Do you believe this is true? If so, what can or should be done about it?

d. Parents who believe a woman's main career is marriage and child rearing and that involvement in the world of work outside the home is secondary will pass these attitudes on to their daughters. One result will be that their daughters will experience more depression and anxiety about meaningless and empty lives after age thirty-five than the daughters of parents who do not have this attitude. Do you believe this is true? If so, what can or should be done about it?

e. Parents who believe a woman's main career is marriage and child rearing and that involvement in the world of work outside the home is secondary will pass these attitudes on to their daughters. One result will be that their daughters will consider the male as head of household and be especially sensitive to their needs about not working or working in a career they approve of. As a result, they will have the better prospects for a happier marriage. Do you believe this is true? Why? Why not?

f. Parents who believe a woman's main career is marriage and child rearing and that involvement in the world of work outside the home is secondary will pass these attitudes on to their daughters. One result will be that their daughters will be suspicious and reject women in high status jobs. Do you believe this is true? Why? Why not?

8. The spokesman for each group reports to the entire group. This is followed by a discussion of and reactions to the conclusions by the entire group. The educator will also distribute a copy of "Future Facts for Females."

9. Each parent is now given a copy of "When I Grow Up, I'd Like To Be _____ (for females)." They are told that the directions are attached and that the scoring is the same as theirs. Parents are encouraged to administer it to their daughters and compare similarities and differences along with the reasons for same.

SCORING INSTRUCTIONS

I. *"I'm Strictly A Female, Female."* Score one point for circling the female figure on items 5, 8, 9, and 10, plus one more point each for the other items if you circled male. This tells the extent to which you stereotype these traditionally stereotyped occupations.

II. *"Honey, I'm Overdrawn" (economic dependence).* Score one point each for disliking high salaried jobs and viewing them as men's work; these are items 1, 3, 4, and 7.

III. *"My, You're So Big and Strong" (physical dependence).* Score one point each for dislike of physical labor and viewing it as best done by men; items 10, 7, and 2.

IV. *"Can I Do Anything More For You?" (role dependence).* Score one point each for liking very much the "serving under orders" jobs (5 and 8) and viewing them as best done by females.

V. *"Silly Little Me" (intellectual dependence).* Score one point each for dislike of intellectually independent jobs or high-level, decision-making career, if these same jobs were viewed as best done by males. Items 1, 3, 4, and 6.

Note: Item II is added for reference value only.

Total your scores and compare them to the scale below.

7 or below — surprisingly free of stereotypes—when did you last send a man flowers?

8 through 12 — you have a possible case of incipient female chauvinism. Check for other symptoms.

13 through 17 — remove your name from the library's waiting list for a copy of the *Total Woman*.

18 or above — you can throw away your copy of the *Total Woman*. You already know it by heart.

FUTURE FACTS FOR FEMALES

1. The Bureau of Labor predicts that nine out of ten women will work for some significant portion of their lives. Marriage and family are not a woman's refuge from the world of work outside, for most single family households are headed by women and about 50 percent of all married women work.

2. The average life expectancy of a woman today is 75 years.
3. Nine out of ten women will marry; eight out of ten will have children; at least six out of ten will work full time outside their homes for up to thirty years.
4. One woman in ten will be widowed before she is fifty and three in ten will be divorced.
5. Only one in three girls plan to go to college.
6. The more education a woman has the more likely she is to be in the labor force.
7. The occupational distribution of women is different from that of men. Women are more apt to be white collar workers, but the jobs they hold are usually less skilled and pay less than those of men.
8. Women are two-fifths of all professional and technical workers but are most likely to be teachers and health workers. In these fields, as in all others, women are less likely to be managers and administrators.
9. There still remains a discrepancy in pay between men and women among full time workers employed throughout 1974. Women's median earnings were less than three-fifths of those of men.
10. One study reported in the *Scientific American*, of wives of graduate students in the Boston area, found that an important predictor of a woman's female-role-ideology—the extent to which she sought gratification through her own achievement—is her perception of her mother's satisfaction with life. Dissatisfied mothers in male-dominated households tend to produce daughters who wish to achieve on their own rather than vicariously.

I'd Like My Daughter To Think About A ———— Career.

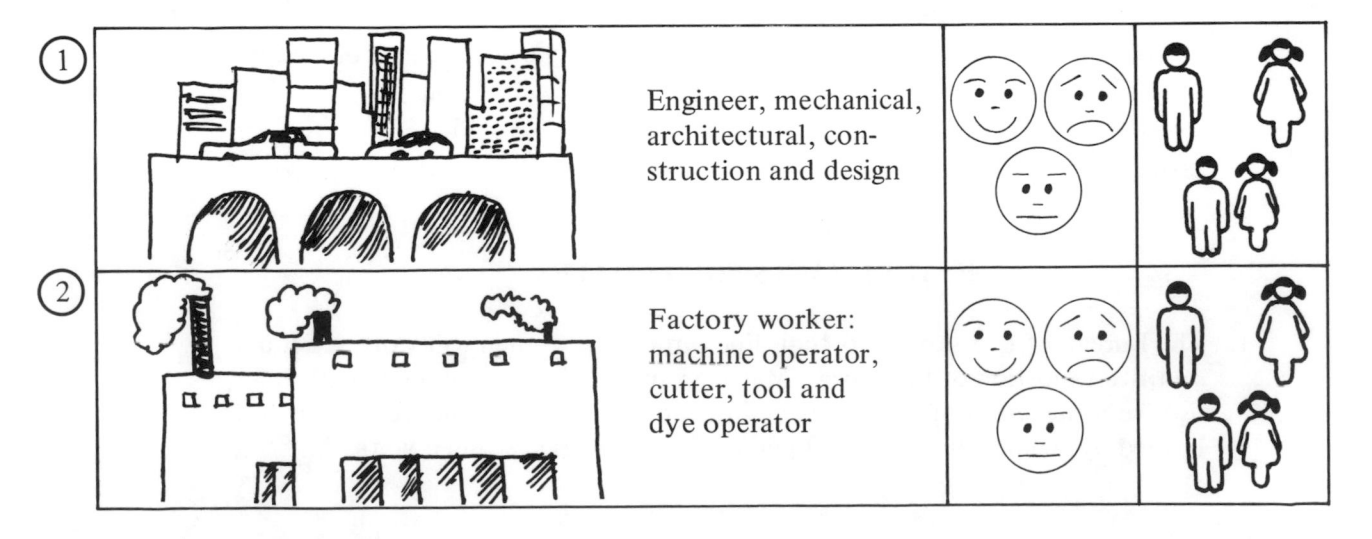

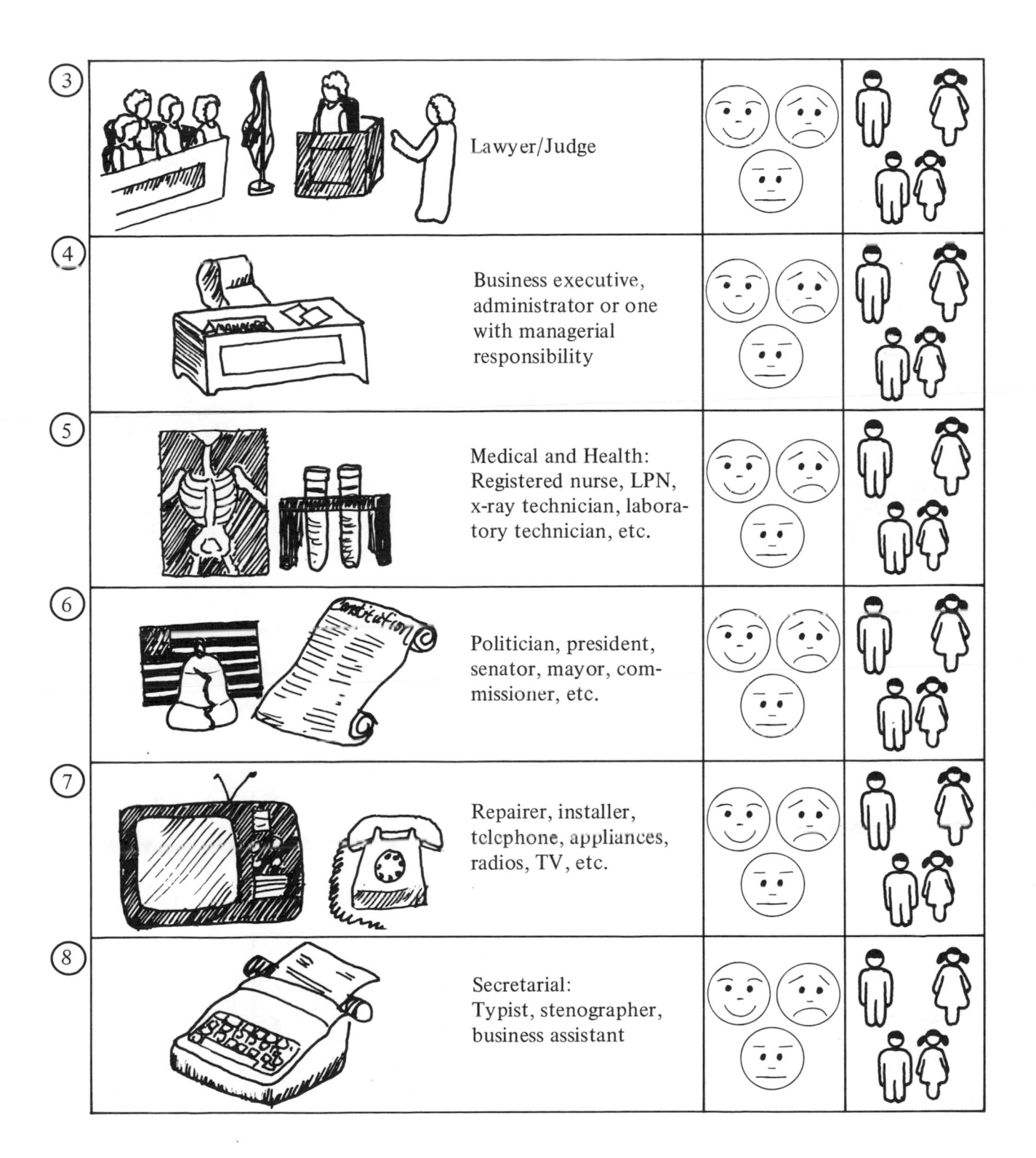

③ Lawyer/Judge

④ Business executive, administrator or one with managerial responsibility

⑤ Medical and Health: Registered nurse, LPN, x-ray technician, laboratory technician, etc.

⑥ Politician, president, senator, mayor, commissioner, etc.

⑦ Repairer, installer, telephone, appliances, radios, TV, etc.

⑧ Secretarial: Typist, stenographer, business assistant

9 	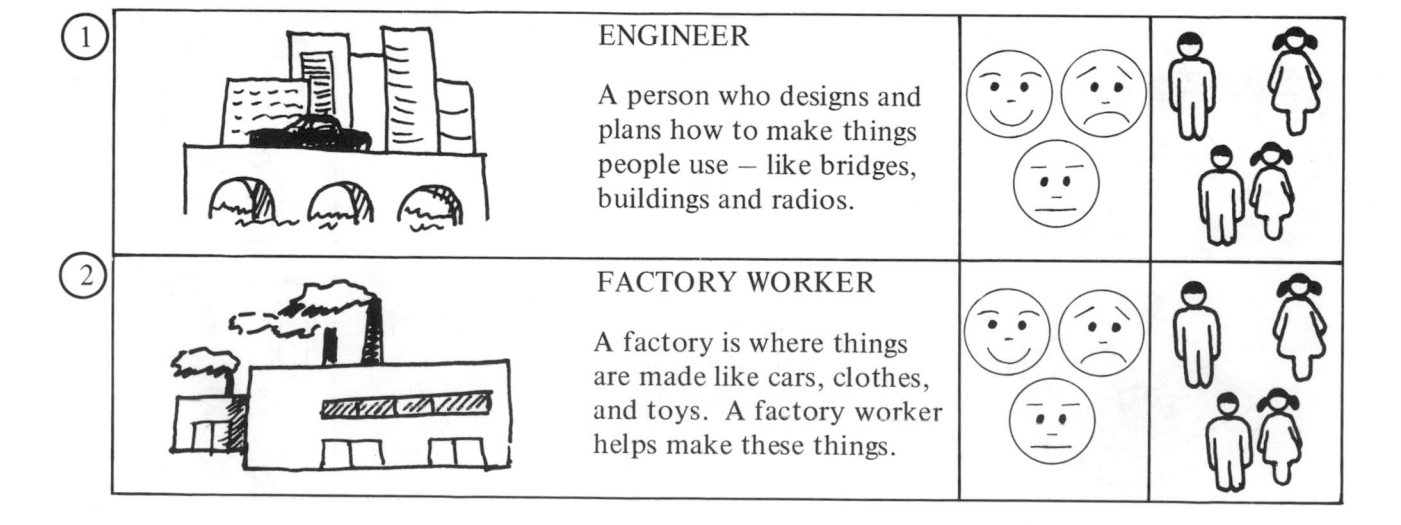	Telephone and switchboard operator	 😊 🙁 😐	 👨 👩 👦 👧
10 		Trucker, teamster	 😊 🙁 😐	 👨 👩 👦 👧
11 		Domestic: house-keeper, babysitter, parents' assistant, homemaker	 😊 🙁 😐	 👨 👩 👦 👧

When I Grow Up I'd Like To Be ——————— (For Females)

1		**ENGINEER** A person who designs and plans how to make things people use — like bridges, buildings and radios.	😊 🙁 😐	👨 👩 👦 👧
2		**FACTORY WORKER** A factory is where things are made like cars, clothes, and toys. A factory worker helps make these things.	😊 🙁 😐	👨 👩 👦 👧

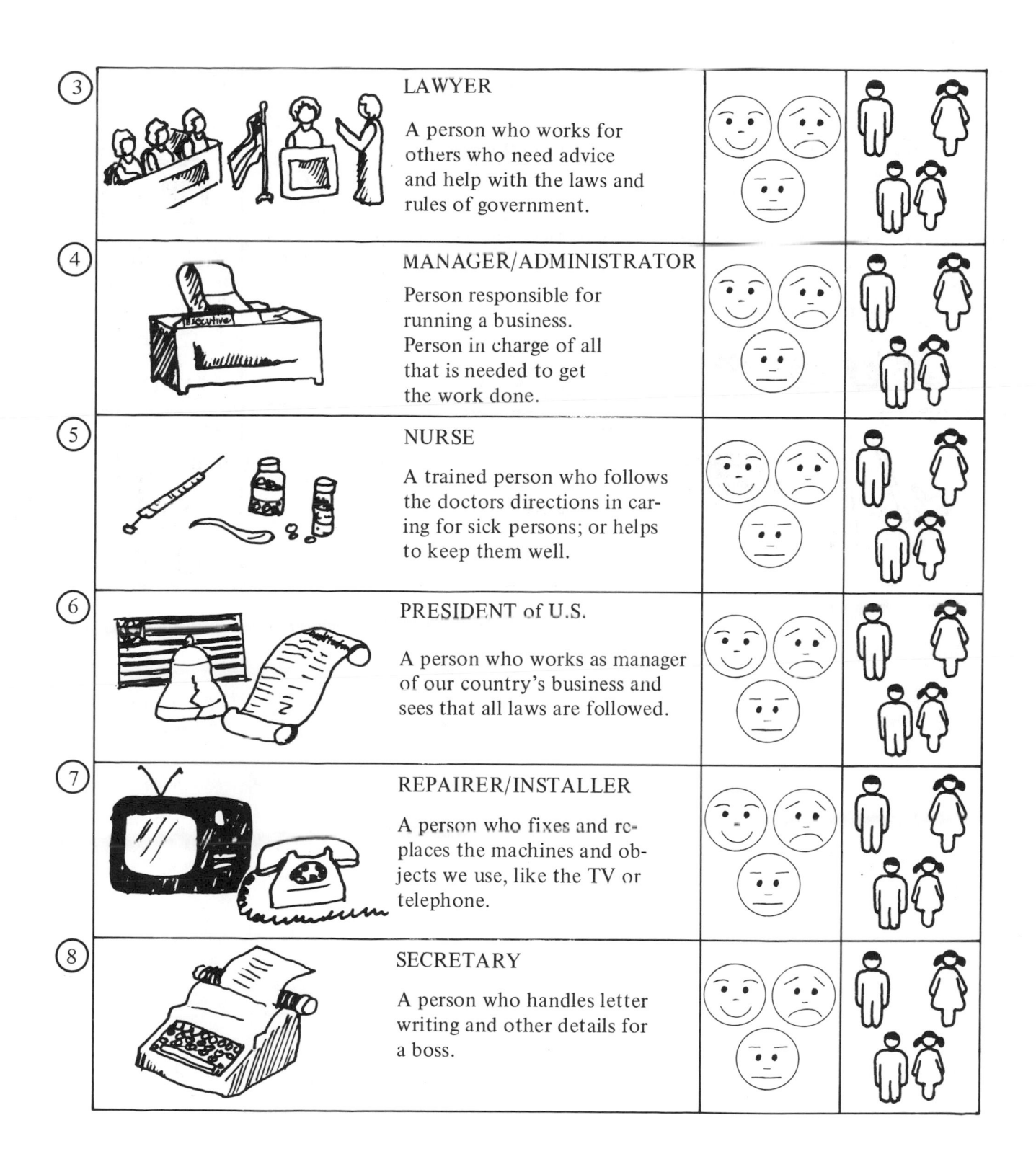

③ **LAWYER**

A person who works for others who need advice and help with the laws and rules of government.

④ **MANAGER/ADMINISTRATOR**

Person responsible for running a business. Person in charge of all that is needed to get the work done.

⑤ **NURSE**

A trained person who follows the doctors directions in caring for sick persons; or helps to keep them well.

⑥ **PRESIDENT of U.S.**

A person who works as manager of our country's business and sees that all laws are followed.

⑦ **REPAIRER/INSTALLER**

A person who fixes and replaces the machines and objects we use, like the TV or telephone.

⑧ **SECRETARY**

A person who handles letter writing and other details for a boss.

⑨		**TELEPHONE OPERATOR** A person who helps people make calls on the telephone. You reach this person by dialing '0'.	
⑩		**TRUCK DRIVER** A person who drives a truck which carries things to people, like food, toys, oil or gravel.	
⑪		**DOMESTIC** A person who keeps house- cleans, cooks babysits, etc.	

Appendix **A**

Excerpts from The Manual Of Developmental Inventory Of Vocational Interest And Sex Role Appropriateness

Purpose:

This inventory seeks to measure the developing vocational interest of young children—grades one through eight—and in addition determines the relationship of occupational interest to perceptions of vocational sex role appropriateness.

It is intended for the classroom teacher's use in acquiring information as a basis for curriculum planning and student guidance. That information is:

1. **Student Perceptions of the Relative Desirability of Occupations.** Rankings may be derived which depict the most to least liked occupations; e.g., 95 percent of all students report that they would not like at all to be a garbage collector.

   Resulting action: The teacher is able to better plan for additional information about the world of work and/or value clarification, such as the dignity of all work.

2. **Amount and Kind of Sex Stereotyping Done by Students.** The teacher is better able to answer such questions as the following:

   What percentage of the (girls) (boys) or (both) perceive being President as a male only job?

   What type jobs do a large percentage of the boys perceive to be feminine? Masculine? Both?

   Do the girls in my class see fewer job opportunities for themselves than for the boys?

Resulting action: The teacher is able to plan more effective activities by particular lessons creating, choosing, or adapting activities directly to student needs.

3.   **Locked-in, locked-out patterned perceptions for both sexes which may prevent further vocational exploration.** For example: Girls frequently see being a pilot as a job they would like very much but one that is more appropriately done by a male. Boys do the same, though not to the same extent, with child care worker.

CRITERIA FOR SELECTION OF 36 OCCUPATIONS
INCLUDED IN INVENTORY

The 36 occupations represented in the inventory were selected to meet the following criteria:

1.   broad coverage of all decile levels in National Average Salary—both men and women. (National Average Salary Statistics reported by the Department of Commerce; U.S. Census 1970),

2.   as broad an occupational area as possible; e.g., factory worker as opposed to press operator, punch operator, sheet metal worker, etc. or engineer rather than the specialities of engineering,

3.   all levels of perceived social status and prestige are represented (almost all 25 of the Deeg and Patterson list of occupations are represented—all but some in modified form). This particular list has been used repeatedly in research on prestige levels of occupations.

4.   representation in all the major occupational classification groups employed in the 1970 Census:

- professional, technical and kindred workers
- sales workers, clerical and kindred workers
- craftsmen and kindred workers
- operatives
- transport workers
- laborers
- service workers
- private household workers

5.   job function descriptions to be comprehensible to age level tested,

6.   at least one member of each of the 36 occupations agreed that the item description was an accurate presentation of the job function (except President of United States).

Administration:

. . . the teacher must see that the second column is folded underneath on each of the four inventory sheets on which the students respond. The students should be instructed not to unfold the answer sheets.

teacher
with class

Before beginning, take a few minutes to be sure that your students understand the concept of job or occupation as including the work a person does on a regular basis to earn money and/or give meaning to their lives. Give one or two illustrations of occupations that are not on the inventory itself and check understanding by listing occupations students tell and describe.

SAY:

PLEASE DON'T TURN BACK THE FOLDED PART ON THE PAPERS I HAVE PUT ON YOUR DESK. WRITE YOUR NAME AT THE TOP OF EACH SHEET. ON THE FIRST PAGE LOOK AT THE FIRST JOB. IT'S A MANAGER OR ADMINISTRATOR. LOOK AT THE PICTURE OF THE PERSON WHO DOES THIS KIND OF JOB WHILE I READ TO YOU WHAT THEY DO. (YOU MAY READ ALONG WITH ME IF YOU LIKE). I WILL READ WHAT EACH JOB IS ABOUT TWO TIMES. Read the job description for item number one twice.

SAY:

IF YOU THINK YOU WOULD LIKE TO DO THIS JOB VERY MUCH WHEN YOU GROW UP, PUT A MARK ON THIS FACE. ☺ (Teacher has drawn the three faces on the blackboard and at this point indicates the happy face both on the blackboard and by holding up an inventory response sheet and pointing to the happy face following item No. 1.) IF YOU THINK THAT YOU WOULD NOT LIKE THIS JOB AT ALL, PUT A MARK ON THIS FACE. ☹ IF YOU ARE NOT SURE OR FEEL IN BE-TWEEN, PUT A MARK ON THIS FACE. 😐 NOW WE WILL GO ON AND DO THE OTHERS. REMEMBER THAT YOU MIGHT LIKE THEM ALL, YOU MIGHT LIKE NONE OF THEM OR JUST NOT BE SURE. WHATEVER YOU THINK AND FEEL IS OK AND YOU SHOULD MARK THAT.

Complete all 36 items with your students. If students are to do complete inventory in one session, continue; otherwise stop here for end of session one.

SAY:

UNFOLD THE LAST COLUMNS ON EACH PAGE. ONCE AGAIN I WILL READ THE DESCRIPTION FOR EACH OCCU-PATION AND THIS TIME YOU WILL ANSWER BY MARKING IN THE LAST COLUMN. LET'S START WITH ITEM ONE, AD-MINISTRATOR/MANAGER (Read the job description again). NOW LOOK OVER AT THE LAST COLUMN. IF YOU THINK

THIS JOB COULD BE DONE BEST BY A MAN, CIRCLE THE
MALE STICK FIGURE. IF YOU THINK THIS JOB COULD
BEST BE DONE BY A WOMAN, CIRCLE THE FEMALE STICK
FIGURE. IF YOU THINK IT COULD BE DONE JUST AS WELL
BY EITHER A MAN OR A WOMAN, CIRCLE BOTH STICK
FIGURES AT THE BOTTOM OF THE BOX.

①		**ADMINISTRATOR/MANAGER** – A person responsible for running a business or organization, like a school or hospital; in charge of all people and material.	
②		**BARBER/HAIR STYLIST** – A person who cuts and fixes hair at a shop.	
③		**CARPENTER** – A person who builds and repairs things made of wood, like houses, tables, furniture and cupboards.	
④		**CHILD CARE WORKER** – A person who works to help young pre-school children to learn and grow; at home, the nursery or anywhere.	
⑤		**DENTIST** – A person who takes care of people's teeth and fixes their cavities.	

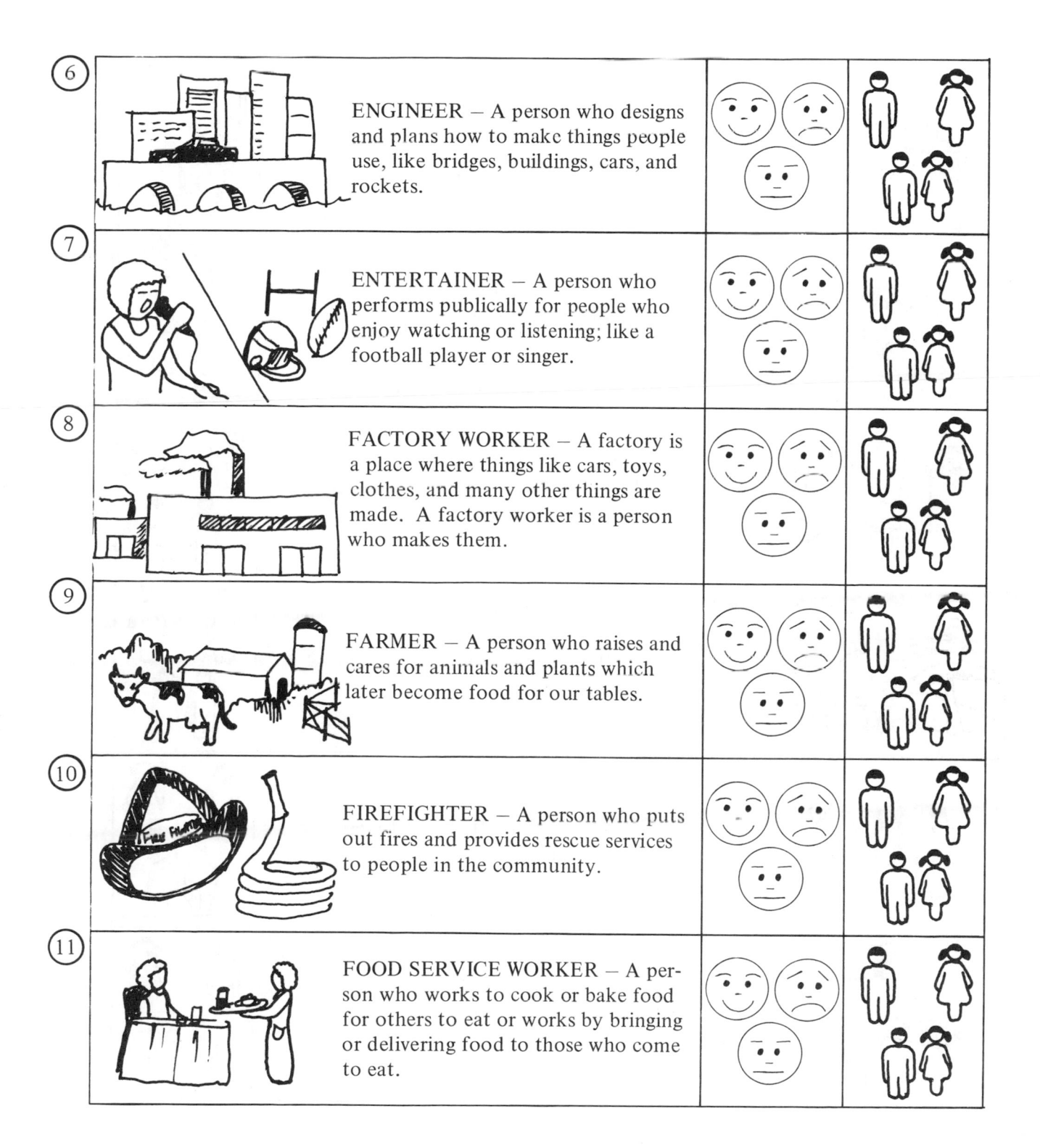

6. ENGINEER – A person who designs and plans how to make things people use, like bridges, buildings, cars, and rockets.

7. ENTERTAINER – A person who performs publically for people who enjoy watching or listening; like a football player or singer.

8. FACTORY WORKER – A factory is a place where things like cars, toys, clothes, and many other things are made. A factory worker is a person who makes them.

9. FARMER – A person who raises and cares for animals and plants which later become food for our tables.

10. FIREFIGHTER – A person who puts out fires and provides rescue services to people in the community.

11. FOOD SERVICE WORKER – A person who works to cook or bake food for others to eat or works by bringing or delivering food to those who come to eat.

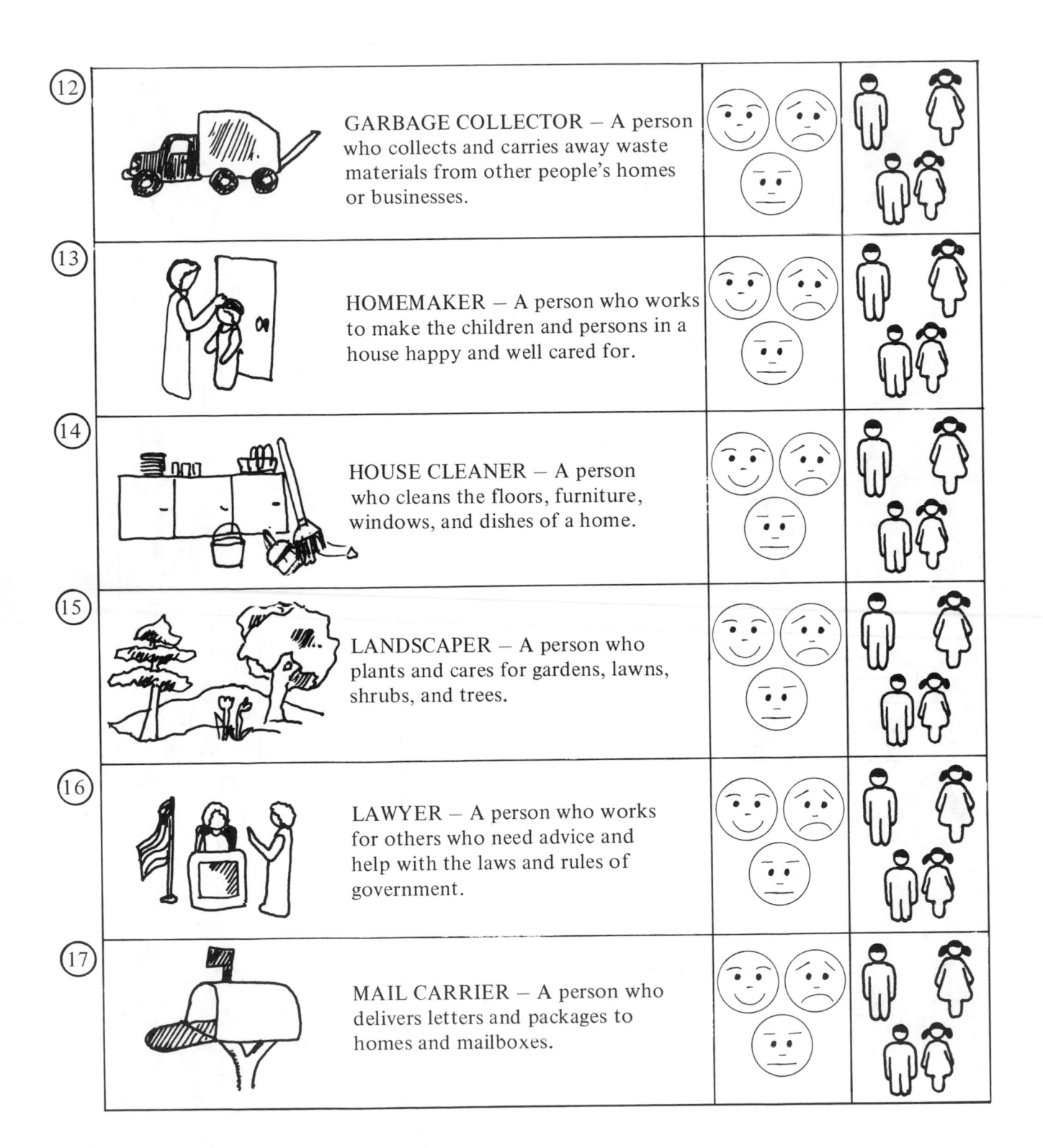

12. GARBAGE COLLECTOR — A person who collects and carries away waste materials from other people's homes or businesses.

13. HOMEMAKER — A person who works to make the children and persons in a house happy and well cared for.

14. HOUSE CLEANER — A person who cleans the floors, furniture, windows, and dishes of a home.

15. LANDSCAPER — A person who plants and cares for gardens, lawns, shrubs, and trees.

16. LAWYER — A person who works for others who need advice and help with the laws and rules of government.

17. MAIL CARRIER — A person who delivers letters and packages to homes and mailboxes.

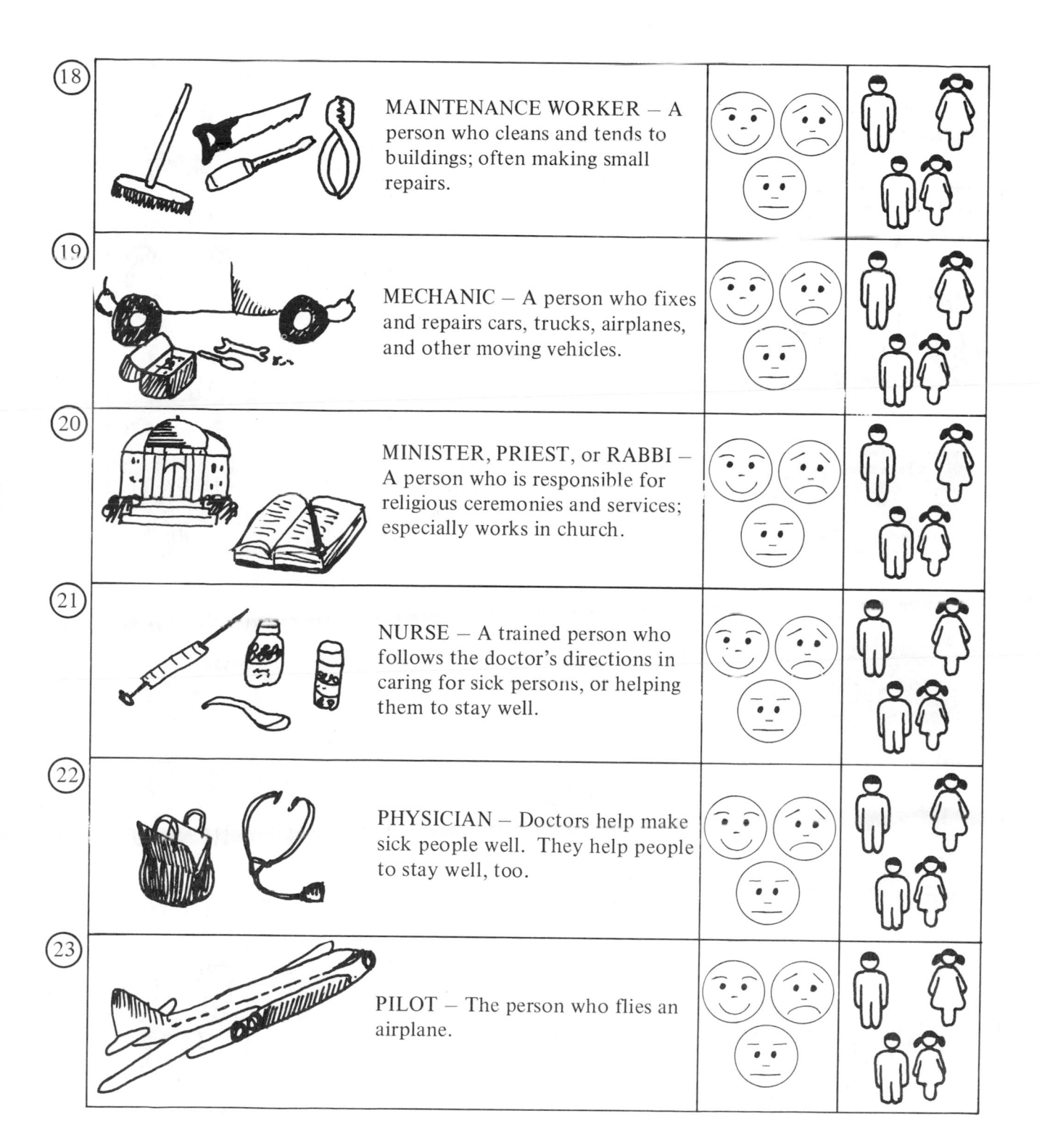

18. MAINTENANCE WORKER – A person who cleans and tends to buildings; often making small repairs.

19. MECHANIC – A person who fixes and repairs cars, trucks, airplanes, and other moving vehicles.

20. MINISTER, PRIEST, or RABBI – A person who is responsible for religious ceremonies and services; especially works in church.

21. NURSE – A trained person who follows the doctor's directions in caring for sick persons, or helping them to stay well.

22. PHYSICIAN – Doctors help make sick people well. They help people to stay well, too.

23. PILOT – The person who flies an airplane.

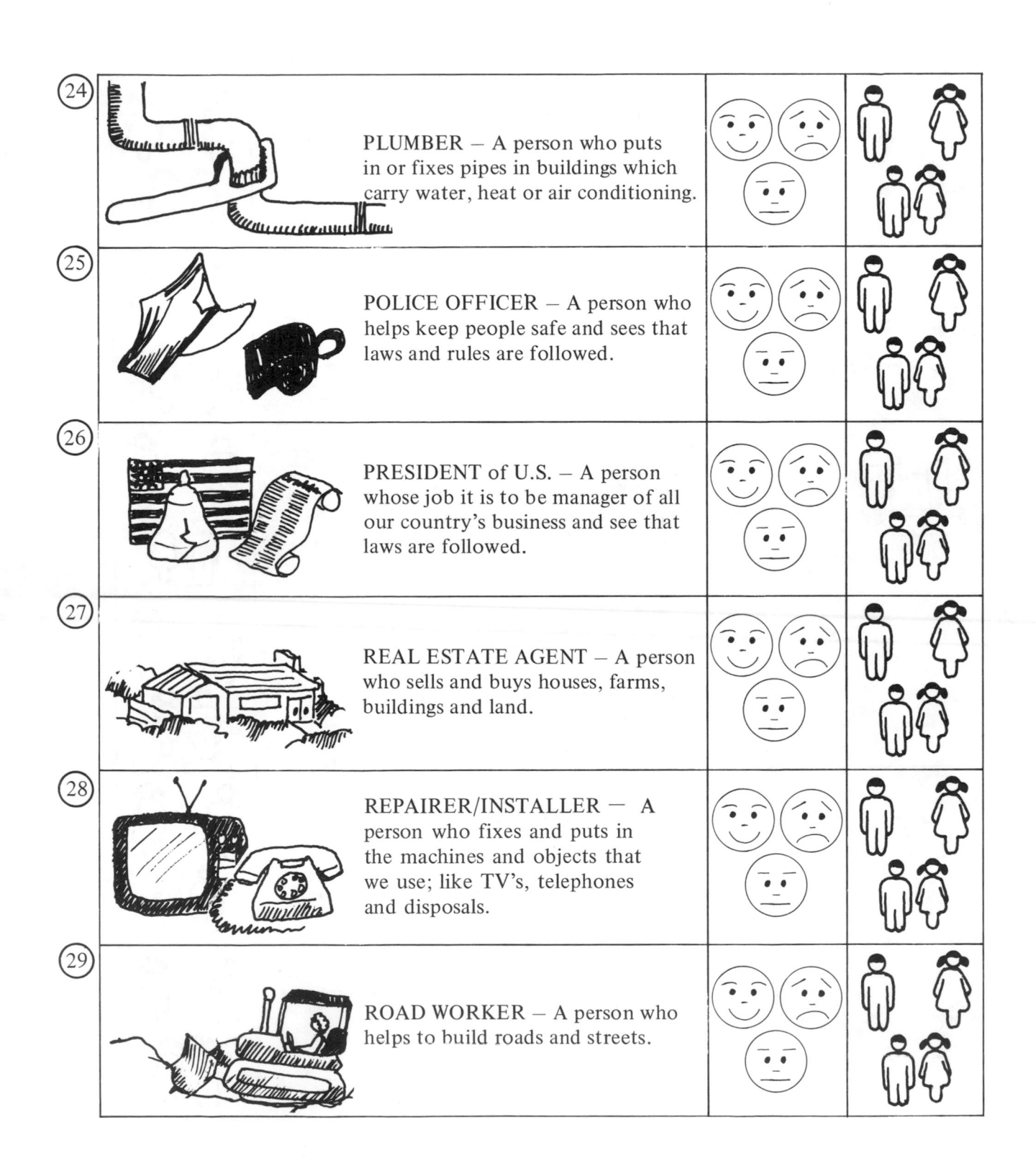

(24) PLUMBER — A person who puts in or fixes pipes in buildings which carry water, heat or air conditioning.

(25) POLICE OFFICER — A person who helps keep people safe and sees that laws and rules are followed.

(26) PRESIDENT of U.S. — A person whose job it is to be manager of all our country's business and see that laws are followed.

(27) REAL ESTATE AGENT — A person who sells and buys houses, farms, buildings and land.

(28) REPAIRER/INSTALLER — A person who fixes and puts in the machines and objects that we use; like TV's, telephones and disposals.

(29) ROAD WORKER — A person who helps to build roads and streets.

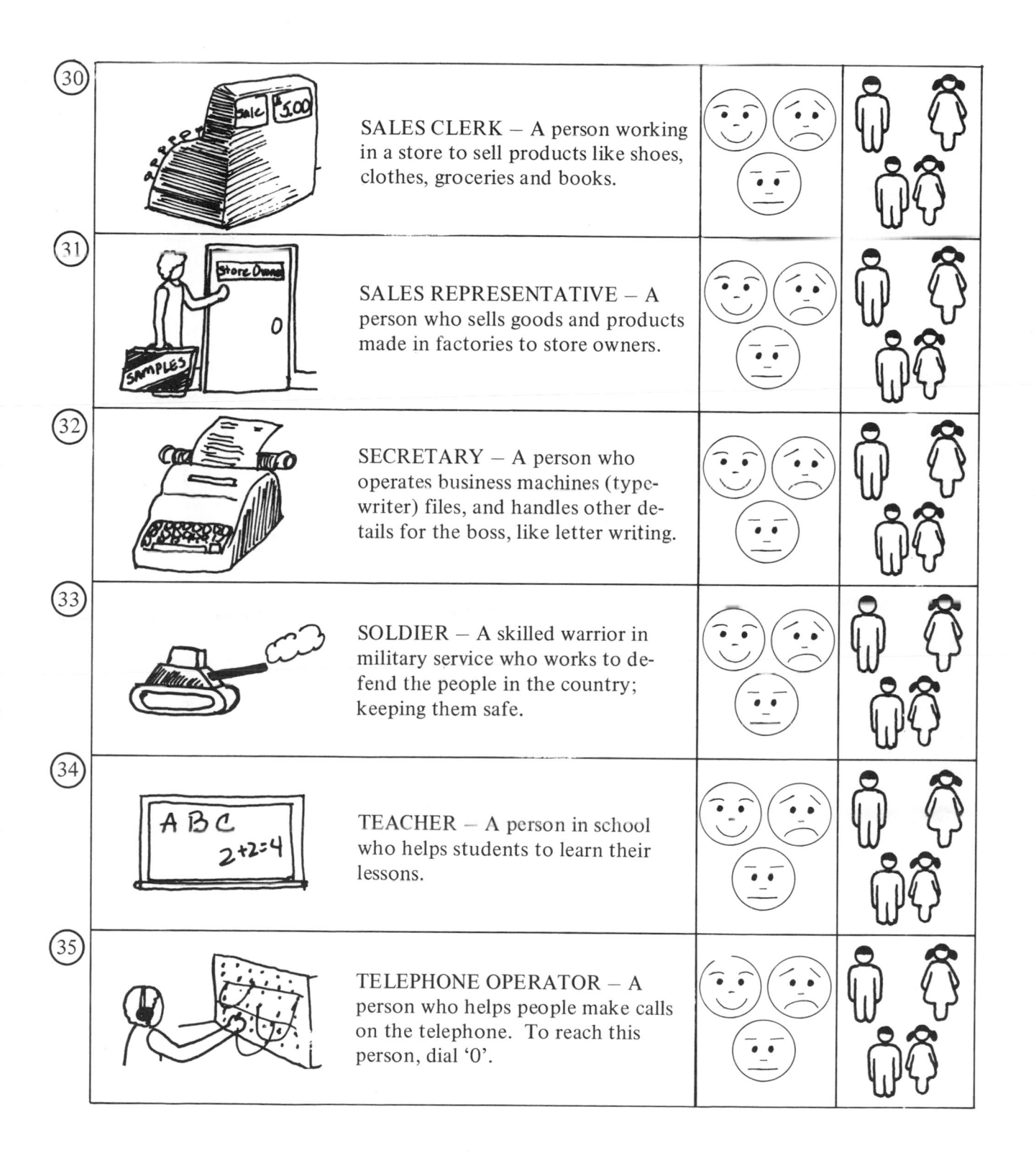

30. SALES CLERK — A person working in a store to sell products like shoes, clothes, groceries and books.

31. SALES REPRESENTATIVE — A person who sells goods and products made in factories to store owners.

32. SECRETARY — A person who operates business machines (type-writer) files, and handles other details for the boss, like letter writing.

33. SOLDIER — A skilled warrior in military service who works to defend the people in the country; keeping them safe.

34. TEACHER — A person in school who helps students to learn their lessons.

35. TELEPHONE OPERATOR — A person who helps people make calls on the telephone. To reach this person, dial '0'.

(36)

TRUCK DRIVER — A person who drives a truck which carries things to people, like food, oil, toys or gravel.